Big thanks to Caroline Hurry, sub-editor who was superb, fun to work with too.

Also a shout-out to all the reviewers who leave reviews for books they enjoy. Without you it would be harder for others to find the good books.

If you think this is a good book, please leave a review.
Thank you.

If you would like to give feedback on the book to the author send a message via Twitter to @tribalideas
- please mention the book name

Please subscribe to the authors daily newsletter here:
https://theauthorityfigure.substack.com/

Contents

Introduction: The good, the bad, and the perfect

Now, for an important announcement

This is a book about growth, it is unusual in that we are going to define negative and positive growth strategies, although the focus of this book is using positive story strategies to ease implementation.

Implementation is key. I can tell you many stories, but the reality is you really want to know how to do this for yourself, my hope is to teach you to fish, so you can fish over and again. The negative stories are included (just in this introduction) to try to highlight what to avoid as soon as possible. The rest of the book is dedicated to practical implementation and, as you may have guessed, the solution is to use the story in your marketing, to make sales and generate profits.

Let me ask you a question : Who are some of the most well-known politicians of our time (this is not about supporting them), this is to make the point of the story? Your answer is likely to include a current or former Prime Minister, President or leader of the Kremlin. They all tell stories. Boris Johnson was an established author and journalist, before he became Prime Minister. The president certainly had his stories, as does just about every other President, and then there were Ukraine and Russian leaders. Most Russian stories we do not believe can be true, but it seems they are believed by the Russian people. The Ukrainian President, Zelensky his story is that he did not want a ride to leave the country, he wanted arms.

OK, so it works in Politics. What about business?

Well, the richest, most successful businessman of this century so far, although it follows most others (notably Trump) is Elon Musk and he tells stories all the time. Sometimes funny, usually controversial and sometimes sued.

When Musk bought Twitter he walked in with a sink, asking the world if it has 'sunk in' yet. He also randomly spouts weird conspiracy theories and was once filmed smoking pot on a podcast. Elon wakes up wanting to be today's story.

In the case of Elon, he is well known not to spend money on advertising, preferring instead to use story as his medium and much of what he has had to say has gone viral, repeatedly, for years. There is a man who has cracked stories.

Elon Musk has gone to lengths many of us would not dream of, but how many of us might dream of having just a tiny percentage of his buying power?

Oddly, it seems he bought Twitter to sell advertising space. Advertising is likely the main revenue model they have and yet he is proud not to advertise himself.

One thing all these story tellers have in common is that they nearly all like a good story and know they are always delivered with a twist. They say and do opposite things. If people expect 'Y' they will do their best to be the opposite 'X'. If you can expect anything, you can expect the unexpected when it comes to good storytelling.

The plot twist heart of all good stories

I wonder if these big names who rely so much on storytelling know it, or if the technique is simply obvious and instinctive to them.

Personally, I started as a young entrepreneur and early on I did a range of publicity stunts. When I was about 25, I had a photograph of me cutting a cake announcing that the business was a year old. I sent it to the local paper and some industry magazines and they printed it! At another time, I wrote a press release and included a sentence to make it clear that I was a young man with an ageist policy - I deliberately hired people over the age of 60 (not sure if you can say this nowadays) as I wanted people with confidence to man the phones. I was subsequently interviewed and appeared on local TV, this then landed me my largest ever client, a bank. Someone who needed to get people like those I was hiring on the phone for them.

The point is, every good story ends with a twist

You will find theories behind some of the stories in this book, and as the author, I write from experience, not to layer the theory, but to provide the inside knowledge of how stories work in practice. I am sure there is much more to write on the subject.

Indeed, I could probably continue this theme and write volume 2.

However, there is a lot here. Like most good things, it changed from being a guide I had written out for some of my consulting, coaching and mentored clients to a full-blown book. Here is the result.

What to avoid: Negative growth stories

A negative growth story is a bad strategy and should be avoided, obviously, we want to grow a business, not shrink it, yet I have a couple of examples of shrinkage - to be avoided.

The classic negative strategy is the pile 'em high and sell 'em cheap strategy. It can work, yet it is hard work. It tends to run dry at the end. The strategy is focused on the more we sell, the more market share we will acquire and so the more competitors we will lock out and so we can own it all.

Growth that does not grow profits is illusionary. Growth without profit is possible, and it can enable the dominance of a market. It is at times employed by certain countries and by emerging players who have capital to burn, but eventually there comes a point where capital has to be repaid.

China Syndrome

For example, we could look towards China, there are other countries on a mission of self destruction, China is the biggest.

Let's call it China syndrome. It is contagious and almost impossible to stop.

China exports many items, with dedicated city ecosystems established. The majority of manufactured output is sold abroad. They are not local consumers of their product and, in many cases, never will be.

China relies on exports and has the added cost of transportation. They have bulk transport systems and certain International Agreements create artificial market opportunities, from when China was an emerging economy.

For example, it is more expensive to post an item from London to Manchester, a shorter distance than from Shanghai to Manchester. The cost of shipping, despite the distance being much longer, is amazingly, thanks to international agreement, cheaper. No wonder companies buy from China.

However, you can tell when the economics of a nation are overblown when that nation prefers to invest overseas. If business was so good, surely they would be putting all their capital time and energy into building more cities and manufacturing infrastructure. Well, China has a few problems, one of which is a declining population.

Have you heard of China's Belt and Road initiative? It is where China lends neighboring countries enormous sums to pay for transport systems. Therefore, transport systems are built to connect to China in some way. A great plan for China and the local country to get access to cash and build the infrastructure needed and get lower cost supplies in the future, faster, potentially, if they are purchased from China. You can see the double win for China. Plus, the way the deals are structured, China will get a lot of income back on those loans for years to come.

It is interesting, as China finances an initiative it also supplies. The neighboring country will forever pay back the debt. If the Chinese manufacturing economy was so good, as a result of the high growth, why should they not invest even more locally, so they can sell more internationally?

The reason is that subsidies ensure that manufacturing and distribution are run at a loss.

When a business makes ever more and then more and then continues to expand and doubles, triples and growth explodes, losses only increase. Yet those losses are covered by cash flow if the company increases sales.

The misleading signals of growth continue to enable subsidies. With ever more money coming in to cover the losses, the problem is hidden. It is not until a 'correction' occurs that it can be seen. Few will admit to loss-making activities. Instead, they will point to market dominance, transformation, jobs and more.

Once a subsidy program starts, it becomes very difficult, there are few who to it turn off.

In the example of China, turning off industrial subsidies would mean equipment would be wasted, potentially millions would become unemployed and costs would mount astronomically, as there would be no income covering the resulting costs at all. In many ways, it has now started. This process cannot stop. However, disasters are starting to come into view.

This is a key reason why these nations are so interested in acquiring the land of their neighbours, and in appropriating land from their own native inhabitants, as land is a hard, indisputable asset. It can be borrowed from and built on.

So it would seem that the near term focus of China has switched to military power and might as the next step is for them to dominate and take control of other peoples' land, potentially. We will see.

However, all of this could be avoided if they were smart and able to change their focus. Change will require much better story telling than the military ones that are set to emerge in China if it continues in its expectation of absolute power.

Avoiding China Syndrome

So this book covers only the other side of growth, the growth strategies that make money.

You can certainly acquire new clients at a discount, you can give people a free trial, and you can let them try before they buy. You can sell discounted products to grow market share. However, you have to know and prepare for the switch, just like there is a switch in the story. There comes a point, when someone appreciates the benefit and discovers there is money to pay if they want to continue.

I have already sowed the seeds for exactly this in the story already told, where this book started out as a guide for my coaching, consulting and mentored clients. In other words, if you like this book and you want me to help you, services are available on a paid for basis and I have laid out how.

This is a strategy presented as a template with transparency for you to take, modify and amend to create profits for your business, not just grow market share. The idea is to win market share and make profits. Take the templates, model them and use them to grow your business in a way that generates new customers and new profits for you.

The templates are not to be confused with copywriting, although in every case, good writing is necessary to persuade, but when you follow a strategy, the idea is to lead someone along a path where the focus is on value, delivery and delight. The objective is to qualify, to genuinely delight our customers and feel comfortable.

Focus on growth with profits

Let's start by being honest with ourselves, businesses large and small need profits to grow and survive.

Funnily enough, those businesses that grow and grow without turning a profit get to a point where the funding stops, and the investors start to realise they have been had. It almost happened with Amazon, who lived on investors' cash for over a decade when it started and a public narrative was well established that it was likely to never make a profit. Therefore, it was with some surprise that one day, Amazon announced small profits.

Amazon had to continually show profits from them on to maintain investment and show it remained worthy and then it was able to deliver bumper profits too.

Amazon have a good problem.

The problem is that Amazon finds itself in many small market niches.

Overall, in the beginning, it was a book reseller. However, all books are different, there are different formats and sizes and media types. For example, e-books, audiobooks, paperbacks and hard cover options.

Each book, both fiction and non-fiction, tends to fit into a different niche.

Customers tend to buy by niche, so Amazon needed to know a lot about its product and also about its growing customer base. It was a business that was very compute-intensive. In short, Amazon has a huge amount of data flowing about. As a result, it learned how to introduce new books to the right readers and do so with a product that has slim margins.

Amazon proves niche customer marketing is not just possible but profitable and provides us with an example of strategy in practice.

Amazon had to continue to generate profits to show it was not a flash in the pan and then it became a real darling of the markets as it seemed to create profits hand over fist. It had a set of profitable growth strategies and, unlike others who had gone before, Amazon, to the relief of investors, was not a flash in the pan.

The value of owning a niche market

It is better to grow with fewer highly qualified, excited and enthusiastic customers than it is to try and please everyone.

Politicians rudely discover they cannot please all the people all the time, at best only half. We know, for instance, even in the world of commodity products, such as trainers, for example, although the markets are large, the best strategies target a certain kind of athlete. So the followers of certain athletes can be like their heroes, and wear the same sportswear.

We see football supporters wearing the football kit of their chosen team.

This is a niche strategy, sometimes a large niche, but niche nonetheless. Niche market strategies do not target everyone. They don't need to.

A country does not need to have one strategy. Indeed, if there is a problem with that strategy, as it seems there is in China, then ultimately, unless they take the time to implement profitable strategies, they are doomed to failure. This is a decision they make for themselves.

Profitable strategies are not difficult, they tend to be more fragmented, as Amazon found. However, this is what happens when you are market driven as opposed to product-driven. There are many more opportunities. Whereas China has dedicated manufacturing cities where the focus on manufacturing is very tight. This leads to product-led manufacturing.

China and businesses who suffer from China syndrome tend to be product-driven.

Going for growth with profit generation

It is hard to put your price up when you are known for being the cheapest in town as many have learned to their cost.

Indeed, there have been many brands have done all they could to reduce costs to become more competitive. FW Woolworths, now a defunct brand, was a multi-generational retail powerhouse with branches across the US and Europe that simply disappeared as in the end it could not make enough profit to service its' debt.

FW Woolworths tried many things. For example, by changing carpet color to brown, the dirt brought into the stores on customers' shoes was disguised and so it meant lower cleaning costs. You can probably sense the smell of a store from this description alone and spot a contributing reason for the unsurprising decline.

On the other hand, a profit-focused growth strategy has identified its customers, knows what they want, is determined to give it to them and be appreciated for it. This, in turn, this enables prices to include profits.

The focus on customer needs fundamentally changes the dynamics of a business in ways you may not expect. Beyond the obvious profit generation, it means an enterprise can become self-funding. An enterprise can earn better returns on it's investment through the creation of profit than can be earned in a bank savings account. More importantly, it can lead to a greater profit than the cost of borrowed money.

When you operate in a niche, your marketing costs are going to be reduced because you know where your customers are or will be at a certain time and at certain places. Rather than need to advertise everywhere, you only need to run promotions in a few places. This means your strategy will be much easier to implement and more creative aimed, spiking genuine interest in your target market.

When you know who you are for and only have to focus on giving them what they want, this saves a packet. It avoids the need for persuasion, which can take time, and is expensive and often produces negative, unintended results.

Knowing who your market is also makes it harder for competitors. For example, why would a competitor try to run a promotion in a space you occupy when perhaps there are other spaces they could target that are clear. The niche market approach is great for attack and defense.

In addition, as you know the numbers, you can easily buy more or even spend more on advertising, as you are certain of the rate of response you will get as you have already determined your expected returns on investment (ROI). You know what you can afford to spend to hold the market and how much it will cost to defend and perhaps retake the market, or enter a new market, making your enterprise much stronger and more effective as a result.

The overriding growth lesson

Sustainable growth is only facilitated by profitable sales.

The payments customers make for the goods and services provided must include a contribution to profit. As a result, an enterprise can increase its' investment in strategy. In turn, we avoid China syndrome.

Indeed, there is a large section of the financial services industry where it is easy to acquire an unending source of finance for a business without giving away a single point of equity. This is called sales financing. This is where you have customers and outstanding unpaid sales invoices.

Banks will take a sales invoice as collateral and give you 95-97% of the face value and keep 3-4% for themselves. Where that 3-4% includes an insurance premium, so in the rare case of a customer going bust you are covered. It also means your customer pays the bank, and they chase the money. You save on administration staff and can always be nice to customers.

My experience was my costs were much higher when I tried to do all these things in-house and, as a business owner / manager, I slept a lot better, as all I was left with was the management of strategies and campaigns to drive more profitable sales and to continue to drive the growth of the business. A solid, long-term solution.

Why are stories key?

All growth strategies follow a plan, it is there in the dictionary definition for all to see.

Your plan becomes your story. Working on the story is, in simple terms, the key to reverse engineering success. You don't start with a story, you start with the market. The first thing you want to know is their story

Now you should try and work out a story as to why that market should love you and your product or service over and above anyone else and why your story will stand out as the natural, first choice. If you had a product or service that could stand out and would be the natural first choice, but your market did not know about it, they would not buy it. That is, where the story comes in.

A story bridges the gap and popular stories, as you may well know, normally have the star of the story. In this case, the star of the story, invariably, is the customer. So the objective of the story is to make the customer look good by delivering, in a unique and special way. When we do that, we have broken the link between price and want. It becomes possible to charge higher prices when your customers are certain they will receive high values.

A well-told story provides perception and carries sufficient proof to make it real to those it is told to.

A simple example story

Try this, it works, here, see for your self.

Stories do not have to be complex. The best stories are generally short ones where we get to the point. There is no need to dial in sophistication.

There are a million ways to tell a story

Much of my time is spent taking stories apart, de-clunking, pulling out the mystery, making them easier to understand. Clever stories tend to confuse people. Less is usually more.

You can tell a clever story in an instant. These are the stories where the only response is ugh? What was that? A good story makes you think: "That's for me" or better: "I want one of those!"

Telling a story in a million ways

The reason you might want to tell a story in many ways is because stories go cold and online many sites (like Twitter) are not happy with duplicate content.

Who knows how many times you could tell a story, it seems so many, conceivably such a high number as a million may not be that unreasonable.

For example, you could take one story, adjust it for the seasons, then for the different types of audience, based on a different time frame and so on. There are so many variables, such as time, place, values, age groups, animal species etc, a million variations become plausible.

There is more to it than duplicate content. For example, take the Dentist example, it could be possible to conjure up a million stories (more or less) to include the word dentist as part of the payoff and you would have many more ways to bring the word into conversation.

To a Dentist and someone who needs one, it is essential to let people know where to go and what to do. Only a good story can reveal the information you want to share or discover in an interesting way. For example, a referral is the result of a good story being told.

Perhaps now is time to tell another story.

Are you sitting comfortably?

Chapter 1: Hook 'em In!

Time to get your spurs!

You can tell stories about anything.

You can tell happy stories that are so funny they are sick. You can go to extremes. However, the format of an extreme story is much the same as a mild one.

Sometimes extreme stories are corporately acceptable, some are not, most in this book are frameworks, which means you can plug in your own content, determine your own extremities.

What follows is a story that many will find amusing, and a few will consider unsuitable, it all comes down to your values and application. It is merely an example of a story that most will understand.

This might be a story you may want to adapt, expand or go deeper if you are targeting young men. I use this story as a simple way to show where we could go with the story, one direction that would appeal to the target audience and, indeed, has been tested over and over the world over.

I have changed the names and places to protect the innocent.

Why Your stories Suck

You may think your life is boring and uneventful, but this proves you really can make a story out of anything.

You must prepare first.

The essence of a good story is preparation.

Your preparation is the setup

The setup should be one or two sentences at most.

"So I headed downtown to get my haircut..."

No need for more information, let the reader imagine themselves heading into their own town.

Create a breadcrumb of clues

"As I walked into town I realized it was getting dark. I usually carry a torch, but not tonight"

The reader starts to become intrigued

No reason to explain why. Less is more.

Character makeup

Ideally, we want to highlight a personality trait and put the character among other characters, as this widens the interest.

"I will meet Steve along the way and he is always fun as he only has eyes for women, beer and football."

Now, you have met Steve and you have an instant three word picture of him.

Positioning

People care about themselves more than anything else, so you want to show your readers a place or thing they would recognize (politicians use this all the time).

You could go for a town or city, weather, or workplace, for instance

You will have the best response if you talk to Londoners, for instance, about something that is known about London. Say the Tube. (The Tube is the underground transport system)

Or Californian sunshine rather than a tax on Californians.

Pivot

A story that does not pivot is just a description

The pivot breaks the pattern.

Chances are your reader expects it.

Make it fun.

People will have fun if you are.

Possible outcome

I can't just leave you hanging.

As ever, Steve spots some girls.

We go for a beer, we watch football and yet again I don't manage to get my haircut.

Do girls just like football-loving, beer-drinking men with long hair?

Strategy & Tactics

An experienced author knows a story follows a strategy where the objective is to attract a reader, pose some intriguing questions and encourage the reader to read on. First, a writer needs to learn how to write and just like learning to ride a horse, it takes practice. At first you may well head nowhere and just go around and around the paddock, where staying on the horse may be the biggest achievement.

It seems to me most enterprises are still learning to ride the horse that is social media. Aimlessly, going around the paddock, learning to ride. Which is a great place to start, it needs to be done. However, at some point there comes a time to leave the paddock and to start traveling somewhere. The story changes, as will your strategy.

Similarly, you may open a Twitter account because you want to follow Elon Musk, or perhaps you see some other point of interest to cause you to act.

In the early days you will post random thoughts, spot, and share interesting articles, and generally tag along to see what might interest your followers. The chances are the followers you will attract will be close friends and associates happy to support you and your new enterprise.

Many will find it fruitless and may even hand it off to the 'professionals' who will run your social media account for you. It will probably still be a fruitless exercise, but at least it will be operational, a social media presence exists, it will be ready, poised to take a future important announcement perhaps.

A strategic decision was taken to open an account, but operationally there is no follow through strategy, just a perceived tactical need to post. Your action is akin to getting on that horse, being able to ride, but never leaving the paddock, you are not going anywhere, but you feel perfectly safe, you feel like you are in control, the horse trots when you command it to do so.

Twitter is not the only place you should employ story. Your story should be employed everywhere. I pick on Twitter as it is one of many media platforms that is often devoid of story, or contains, invariably the wrong kind of stories.

The idea behind this book is to demonstrate the many strategies you can employ using story to actively engage with your audience. Through story you can use all the media available and at your disposal whether it is in person, in print or digital. All communications can benefit from story.

The most common story for most enterprises is simply 'buy my stuff' which is one story which works when customers choose to come to you. So commercially then, perhaps the first strategy would be to use story to encourage customers to come to you. Another strategic use of story might be as a method to thank new customers for becoming customers with a view to retaining their custom and to encourage them to buy more. An even better story outcome would be to make sure you thank them every time they buy.

The Trojan Horse

Stories can be funny, happy, sad, they can even carry hidden occupants.

Who has not heard of the Trojan Horse? Nearly every story arrives with hidden occupants. The question is, who are those occupants in your account? What story do you want to tell?

The Trojans are the modern enemy hidden in your network in the contemporary cyber story.

In this book of business stories, the insider message is what story can do for you. All the examples appear to be about the heading and yet each story contains additional meaning and purpose.

Broadly, the bigger purpose is to provide a collection of stories, tips, and frameworks you can use as templates to rewrite or model, to cause your audience to engage with you, so you can hook 'em in.

The key problems that must be faced and overcome

There are two: technical content and content marketing.

Technical content is generally long winded and boring too. So, mistakes are made, or systems are under-utilized, or require expensive training. Of the two issues, technical content is more easily dealt with. Generally, the answer, when it comes to technical content is to be brief, direct, and clear. You will find a couple of chapters dedicated to this key problem in section 2, On Writing.

The other problem, content marketing is much harder to deal with to which the rest of this book is dedicated. There has been an almost universal pivot to content marketing, especially since the advent of social media. Where marketing is often outsourced and meaningless, done because it must be. Often consisting of a few quotes or phrases which tend to focus on being, authenticity, living our best life, or ecology, demonstrating our green credentials and diversity.

I am not against any of those, or to being a good citizen in some way, great sentiments. The problem is they are largely cliched and increasingly dismissed. They are excuses for content. They have wider value perhaps, yet they are generic and can be found increasingly, everywhere. This is the kind of content so universal it is easy to outsource, and no one can really complain about. Without story, it is difficult to actively engage with.

This is already a global billion-dollar industry and set to become multi-billion as we off-shore even more. Problem is, most of it is thoughtless. Not that people are brain dead who do the work, it is largely they are managed poorly, without much direction and they are often paid per item or per hour. We could do with less quantity and more original thinking.

Some of these companies will go the extra mile and find relevant articles and link to them. Having worked with a good number of clients and reviewed thousands of accounts it is a dependable fact that few new followers are found and invariably there is no return on investment at all. Multi-billions are set to be wasted. I am surprised they have not already been found out. We have the capability, we have the media, we have the willingness, and the money is being spent. Why is so much being wasted?

More campaign thinking is about thinking different to paraphrase Apple. We want heads to turn and for consumers to engage, not glance, dismiss and move on. We can't be about filling up space, we must be about getting return on investment and triggering engagement. Good storytelling can do that.

This book is full of stories for you to model. With some suggestions as to how to go about writing them, you will find a range of different types of stories you can tell and a range of angles you can employ. These are all to be found in the first part of the book, part 1: Essential Stories.

There should be enough here for everyone. I would love to get your feedback, let me know via Twitter @tribalideas and if there is more you need, I will try to help you. However, there is more to be found in part two of this book which is about the mechanics of storytelling. In part three you will find several chapters dedicated to writing founders stories. Indeed, you can run your entire future on founder stories alone, provided you deliver value to your reader and apply the Trojan Horse technique of ensuring there is a good story within your good story.

What is your unique perspective?

As you read through this book you may discover there are hundreds of twists and turns available to you. I want to give you a key to unlock many doors and help you stand apart. It is part of a training program I have developed for my Authority Figure clients. The value of this key depends on your answer to this question: What is your unique perspective? When you consider an opportunity, or third-party news release what do you see through your unique perspective lens? As this is how you will add value. This will cause people to want to engage, to look out for you. It will mean you produce less. It should also mean you spend less. Chances are you will get much more back in return. Is it worth it? For every customer I know who has taken this seriously it is. Afterall, your unique perspective is the reason your existing customers do business with you, they expect it.

The surprising truth

A key benefit of story is few question the contents. We are used to taking stories at face value.

A classic story I have heard told many times happened to me. A Brother laser printer I owned broke. I bought it from Amazon a few years ago. When it broke, I sent them an email, expecting to pay for a repair or buy a new one. I was staggered to discover they would send me another.

I could send the old one back in the new packaging if I wanted or dispose of the old one myself locally. I chose to send it back without charge. Of course, I was delighted with the service.

This true story demonstrates story is more powerful than the lame statement 100% no quibble five-year guarantee, which I had forgotten entirely. Luckily, I did not have to ask for it.

Lead with the lesson

Parents know the best way to teach kids is to turn the lesson into a story.

Can it be a fight to the death?

Consider the bible. Over the centuries, many have fought and died for stories.

Form a connection

When you connect with a story, you form a bond because of the shared experience of being a storyteller and story listener. You also set a specific hierarchy level and build trust. You become known for something. If your story was shared, chances are you would be name checked as the person who told the story.

Great for PR, great for referral business.

I heard a story decades ago from Michael Basch, founder of Fedex. I remember being in Los Angeles with about a hundred other men thinking this would be emotional. After all this time I can't recall the hotel or the long and arduous journey from London, just the story.

I remember consciously listening to Michael and knowing what was coming as he spoke. Despite that, I cried with the best of them.

I was aware of the story before. I knew the story was powerful. Yet a room full of grown men all cried. Amazing. Stories can paint pictures. You can ask your listener to add their facts as Michael did to make it real, to add credibility. You can evoke a wide range of emotions in the story: happiness, sadness, joy, and hope for the future.

The best sales presentations I have attended manage to include all the above. A good story can deliver trust and make sales too. No one is left behind.

What can we learn?

The idea of the story is certainly not new; it is not particularly sophisticated. We can employ a wide variety of stories, they are readily available to us, in constant flow, there will never be a shortage.

Stories are common, use and application are easily missed. In our rush to deal with story and different technologies, starting with print, radio, tv, film, the internet, websites, search, social media, AI, and machine learning, we can lose focus on the story itself and focus instead too much on the mechanics of the technology. It is not surprising, technology and what we can do with it is fascinating and we get attracted to technological story!

The media is a conveyor of stories. We need to make sure we use the full facet of story across the media we choose to use. Interestingly, when we ignore the story, we find it hard to recall what we have just heard even minutes later due to our general need for speed.

Yet, suppose we could take a moment to dial it back and invest in a developing story or consider better ways to apply our story, the stories we already have. In that case, we could make search, social media, print, video, TV, film, AI, and machine learning work better for us.

It is true, it is possible. If we can convey an interesting and worthwhile story. A story that shares our angle and delivers value to the recipient, across our media of choice, or, all media, we will have more winners.

We would reach more people at a deeper level. Either our costs would go down, or we could achieve a wider distribution and bigger return on our investment for the same money. Two very ecologically sound and sustainable achievements. Who wouldn't want those?

The simple formula

So yes, stories have a simple, basic, not particularly sophisticated formula.

Stories have a beginning, middle, and end. 3 Acts, you could say. Storytelling techniques found in plays, films, and TV tend to be more sophisticated.

The 3-part story is a sensible place to start. It keeps life simple for our potential clients and us, too. We don't want to get so far into the story that we lose the message.

Therefore, here is how the story will play out for most. Start with a message you want to convey. Do you want to sell more? Help people make better choices or nudge them toward a particular conclusion? Message first. Second: story. The story carries your message. Your message should include the action you want your reader to take.

Then there is the media. Media (print, TV, Internet, etc.) delivers the story that conveys your message.

Both consumer and business markets work in this way.

There is nothing wrong with a simple formula. If anything, a simple formula points to low-cost opportunity and makes application a reality, a genuine practical possibility.

Of course, we can make stories much more sophisticated, there is much more finesse we could add, and there are story genres too. In turn, millions of books are available to buy. However, most of these are very sophisticated and can easily confuse. The last thing we want to do is confuse our buyers; a confused buyer does not buy and will not take any action.

The use of stories is time-tested to engage, drive, motivate, and spur people on to action. However, in the main, we seem to have forgotten about the story part. In the main, in my experience, most advertising agencies and media agencies count the number of packets of information traveling about. Which is nice, yet largely pointless.

In many ways, stories can be a magnificent differentiator. Most of us love stories because stories don't have to be expensive to put to good use. A story does not need to be highly polished and produced. Neighbors can tell a story over a back-garden fence.

Story does not require a big budget, story requires thought. A story has the advantage for startups as they work one on one and for established enterprises who can pay for media who want to either scale or get their message out fast.

Buy time.

Spur customers on with a story.

A story's growth strategy is to motivate your customers.

By telling stories, you can create reasons for customers to act and, in turn, increase sales.

Story represents a significant growth opportunity, is accessible, is easy to implement, yet is demonstrably ignored by most.

I hope I have said enough to motivate you to investigate further. One day, will I hear your story?

The business advantage/The Founder's Tale

Your reader is your live wire.

A story inspires action. The difference is noticeable as readers feel inspired to act on what they read.

Our readers will learn, discover, overcome, and deal with an issue in our business story. We look for readers who have problems to overcome, particularly in non-fiction. In non-fiction, it is easy for us to use the title of our story to define the problem or the solution. Either way, the title or story headline helps the reader grasp the content briefly and calls out a specific interest, like the proverbial dog whistle. It is referred to as dog whistle marketing in the trade.

An enterprise provides stories for prospective clients to engage with as potential customers anticipate finding a solution. Therefore, it will save a lot of time if you determine who your prospective clients are and the problems you can solve before you start. How and why is your service or product delivered to them? This is golden information to help you write your story to meet their expectations.

The answer may be a very small percentage of the total market. That's the point, it is rare that our enterprise will solve all problems, instead it is more likely we can help solve certain issues for certain people who find themselves in specific circumstances.

Your golden story is how you help your clients solve their problems. The founders' story is the classic story most founders tell as the reason they started the business.

The founders' story describes a problem. The founders' experience is how the founder solved the problem, rescued someone who was in trouble, and how everyone lived happily after. This provided the founder with the idea for this business, now established. You could use this as the template for writing your founder's story.

The founders' story is the most valuable story most businesses possess. The last part of this book is dedicated exclusively to the founders' story in order to provide further insights and tools for you.

Your secret weapon

For decades, I struggled to find different ways to describe what I did to keep it interesting for my clients. In the end, I discovered, largely through persistence, the solution was to tell the story from different angles. Which is great until you run out of angles.

I found it harder and harder to find an angle until, in the end, I was clutching at straws. However, each straw was so valuable, it was worth the effort. Eventually, I wrote them out and made some discoveries. Here are a few things I learned:

Daily customer acquisition

Look out and listen in for one new angle, one new story, every day. Consider each conversation you have and review for more new reasons why. The reasons don't have to relate to your business. The trick is to listen in and imagine how they might.

Customer satisfaction

Understand more about what customers get from you. Customers don't just buy on price, otherwise, customers would always buy the cheapest. Customers are more concerned with their feelings, relationships, and expectations than hard facts.

Customer retention

A sale is the beginning of a new cycle. Handled badly, sales can become undone. Managed carefully, more can often be sold. There are at least 6 stories you need to tell clients to reassure them that they have made a great decision (all are contained in a dedicated chapter in part 2: On Writing).

Your success blueprint

The benefits of story are multiple, and they are universally accepted.

Stories drive emotions and convey information across all media. All these elements become part of your success story blueprint. Growth strategies and new products and services are generally best introduced, explained, and demonstrated to others through the power of stories.

The objective of this book and the membership site that supports this book is to provide readers with growth strategy blueprints and real-world applications involving the story.

Much of it works on a fill-in-the-blanks basis. You are given a prompt and invited to write your answers, which do not have to be correct. It is all about getting started.

Every story has a beginning, a middle, and an end. The beginning defines a purpose to read the rest and means you are one-third of the way there. Carry on.

The process is a system of refinement where you start with a loose objective or idea and consider it more as a whole as the whole appears to you.

American novelist Flannery O'Connor stated, "I write because I don't know what I think until I read what I say."

Put your ideas down so you can think about them and refine them for clarity or expand on them.

Sometimes, the best way is to record a Q and A conversation with a colleague.

I urge you to take notes as you go through the chapters of this book and think about growth strategies and how you will use storytelling as your blueprint for growth. One of the great things about stories is you can use them repeatedly to develop your business. Your stories become unique to you, they become valued assets.

So why not start as you mean to go on and take your phone to make a recording or grab a piece of paper and write down your initial thoughts on the elements that are likely to be important in your next story. Most importantly, think about the actions you would like those who engage in your story to take. Do you want them to buy something? Now work backward. Buy what? Why buy that? For how much? Spur your business forward. Go get 'em!

Part 1: Essential Stories

Chapter 2:
5 ways to build a story on what your business offers your clients and why you must

New age demands

There is a big difference in the outlook of life depending on age. Outlook affects business.

The under 40s have spent their whole lives digitally. They see it as part of their lives. The over 40s see digital in a different way, they see digital as something that comes afterwards, life was experienced first.

The under 40s expect to have more experience than goods. For instance, they take an Uber, rather than buy a car. They will see a product as deficient if it does not have a digital component like an app to go with it. They expect everything to be digitally managed, controlled.

The under 40s may invest in a superior product just because one has the more advanced features of an app and the other, better product does not.

Celebrate delivery

Make an event out of the purchasing experience.

When we buy in a shop, we just get a receipt. When you buy through eBay, you have the excitement of winning an auction and eBay makes you certain to congratulate the buyer accordingly. Yet the product is usually second-hand!

The celebration helps to cement customer satisfaction and reduce customer remorse.

Embed digital into the product

Digital components can add a whole new dimension to your product or service.

You don't just buy a Tesla; you get a connected supercomputer for your car to rock! Bicycles are starting to be delivered this way.

What exciting new digital story can you add to your product offering?

New income streams

Add value and charge more, more often with a digital story.

Turning a sale into a subscription has transformed the economics of phones and software. Apple and Adobe are two of the largest businesses on the planet because of regular, monthly, subscription income.

If your business is in a leadership position, perhaps through thought leadership, then the chances are you already have free channels and you produce communications to suit. There is nothing to stop you from expanding or combining these into books or paid for subscription newsletters that will serve to further support your position and, in exchange for making information publicly available, generate an income too.

Digital information (story) sharing is a fast way to maintain market leadership in your field as well as developing new digital-only control systems and services.

Deliver services, not things

A huge percentage of what you buy are not things anymore. They are largely to do with living, from food, rates, to mortgage repayments and what's left tends to be spent on entertainment.

All these observations are about the story of our lives.

Beforehand, in Putin's time, it was all about land grabs and having more than others. In the time ahead, it is all about the simplicity of enjoying and living our lives. We leave the rat race to the rats.

We have not got softer; we have become smarter. It is no longer about having more than another, the have and the have nots. Life is more about enjoyment and simple pleasures. The more we can build enjoyable stories into our lives, the more we can expect to talk about, share, and get business by referral.

We all want a better story.

The emphasis here is on digital experiences, yet experience does not have to be digital.

If you operate an existing business, there is nothing to stop you from celebrating a sale in a different way. For instance, in retail, you could prepare a sample box as a gift, just look at the way perfume is sold. When you buy the main item, you are gifted with unadvertised extras, potentially including a gift box for which your customers are most likely to be delighted.

In addition, I have seen children rewarded with boiled sweets and those who spend above certain amounts rewarded with gift vouchers so they can spend again. There are many ways to celebrate a sale and every opportunity should be taken if you want to put experience at the heart of your business, which is clearly what the winners do.

Service businesses succeed most when they create a real social network around their businesses. Social networks foster connected friendships, which makes it very difficult for people to jump ships or switch horses. Two events the service industry is acutely aware of are easily fixed through the genuine stories connected by true friendships developed over time.

In the long run, the more you can add a digital component to your offering, the better things will get for you as it will be expected by your clients and, indeed, your competitors will use it as a differentiator which could well be an attractive feature to a new client who cannot tell that your overall service package or product delivery is superior.

One of the easiest ways to add digital is through the application of stories which can apply to retail as much as business to business. I was shopping in a store today and while inside I could hear music playing and instead of a DJ there were product and usage tips shared that no doubt served to remind shoppers of things to buy and encouraged purchase for consumption.

Everywhere you go, stories are being told anyway. Why not tell them on-line too. It could well be a fast way of creating an app if your business does not already have one.

Chapter 3: Kick-start your business growth and feel great with these 14 love story sparklers

Every presentation, every business development book, and training course insist that you tell a story to get your message across. It's good advice. I provide the exact same advice; except I am going to show you how to put love in your story, so everyone feels good about learning more.

Your story will have the most impact and generate the deep connections necessary for your audience to take the action you recommend. Testimony to the power story, Bill Clinton, Barrack Obama, and JFK are all known for telling one story that transformed their careers and made them icons in their own time. To many, those presidents remain icons. They were expert storytellers as they knew where to apply the love, let's break it down.

The hard love of home truths

Including your love in a story can mean you have to tell the truth for your big conclusion to have an impact. The harder the home truth, the bigger the impact, the bigger the love you are likely to generate.

However, it is not transactional. You cannot just get to the big outcome by first telling the big bad news. In fact, if you open with huge negatives, you may well get thrown out before getting far at all. The objective is to make a transformation, so the first thing you need to do is earn the right to speak and start by recognizing who you are to be telling your story.

In my case, I had an ordinary, if anything, rough education, as a family, we moved around a lot. At the end of High School, through the magic of showing interest and enthusiasm, I managed to win an apprenticeship. I was interested and enthusiastic as I knew if my application was successful, I would get paid to go to college and study the subjects I had hoped to study anyway. I pretty much told the interviewers. Imagine my amazement when I was selected from a pool of 500 other applicants. I was not special, although I must admit, winning like that, did make me feel special.

Three years later, with certificates and fresh qualifications, I finally clocked in for work. I was so grateful to the company for putting me through college, my enthusiasm and excitement for what they had done for me carried me through. I was excited, I was enthusiastic, I was more than interested, and I was in love with them. Why not, it was not a lot of money, but for a kid who had nothing, to get paid, and then to study the courses studied, it was everything!

And now for the difficult part

Can you see how this story might fill your heart and how you might see yourself in this story? How good would you feel if all that had happened to you? Even if it did not, it is nice to know it is a possibility.

If this story was about achievement, you would probably agree that I have earned my right to speak. Yet I must tell you, having an income nearly killed me. You see, before I bought a car, first I bought a moped and then I bought a motorbike and one rainy day my bike slipped from under me, and I went flying. I landed heavily, under a bus. With broken bones, I was taken away in an ambulance. It was a painful recovery, yet I carried on putting in the hours and I managed to pass my exams, and eventually, I completely recovered.

In this case, the difficult part is about me and how an accident could have changed the course of events. Nevertheless, persistence paid off. I could easily include mention of my hard-working, worried parents and the support provided by the company, who paid for everything, and the love I felt for one and all in the circumstances.

An expanded story to touch the heart

This story could have been because I won an apprenticeship and got paid to go to college and one day, I had a road traffic accident. Despite that, I qualified as per the plan. An equally true story, just with a lot less power. This version contains none of the love that really adds to the story. Why include love? We want to connect with our audience.

Mirroring

To a large extent, I mirrored my reader. You are either reading this at school or have attended school in the past. So, to talk about my time at school is to talk about a place you have attended. After school, we all have choices, an apprenticeship was either available to you or not, or perhaps your experience was similar in that you won a scholarship, or you went to further education without winning any kind of ship, or you went to work. All scenarios are covered.

Audiences tend to want to picture themselves in the story as the storyteller and feel the emotions conjured up as the story unfolds. Mirroring creates the perception that the author has been there for real and has their interests at heart, especially as the story starts by revealing personality traits such as excitement, enthusiasm, interest, and amazement, emotional feelings we all feel, which helps make the story worth listening to.

Context, emotion, and impact

This short story importantly conveyed context. Although there was no description of the school, no reference to the location, or the facilities.

Where it is and what it looked like is entirely in the mind of the reader, you probably imagined a school you have been to, either as a child yourself or as an adult or parent.

Those personality traits mentioned as excitement, enthusiasm, interest, and amazement are all emotions and can be expressed in many ways, including within business stories, business events. This story is yet to conclude and so there is scant mention of business to start with. I was careful also to touch on the higher value of transformation, to counterbalance the transactional, and to appeal to a higher level in the readers' mind, this is both an emotional and impact trigger.

Although, ultimately, most readers will be interested in what happened, The cause and the effect. The possible recruitment to the landing of the apprenticeship. Income transformed into transport. Transport transformed into pain. Pain transformed into success and a career, the result, the ultimate payoff.

Have I attracted your attention?

Just an ordinary person, doing an ordinary thing. What is the likelihood you would be interested in hearing more about this story?

Use A template

You may need some help working out your love story, so a simple template would be a practical place to start.

The objective is always to put your customer at the center of your story, so the story must be more about them than you, as this will help other potential customers see how they can be helped. You probably have many stories and that is good, write them all, you can even write stories for clients you don't yet have, as you still need to inspire them about how you can help them, and this template can help you get to reach them.

Here is the template:

Our book/service/product helps business professionals/mums at home/ local householders/parents/business owners/ managers who want to improve/build/start/open by avoiding/escaping/eliminating making poor/ expensive/late decisions/stuff no one wants and creating measurable results/fast solutions.

So, you can see, it is simple. Our 'A' helps 'B' who wants to 'C' by 'D' and 'E'.

A is about our product or service

In A we get straight to the point of what our product or service is, it can be anything really, including a book, I just put that in there, it is applicable, not just a theory, I use this. This process is also a neat method for coming up with headlines, names or descriptions of products, services, and books.

In B, we refer explicitly to our target market

Many people have difficulty with this, they think they can help everyone. The problem is, unless we are explicit, we help no one.

So, you must consider your target market and you might come up with several, which is why several are shown in the example template. This is a very practical process. Essentially, you write this template for each target market. The idea is, when you meet someone in the target market, or if you advertise to them, you show the most appropriate version.

There is a non-technical marketing term called dog whistle marketing, where we say or announce something that is specifically designed to only resonate with a specific target market. There are certain people among the wider population who are more likely to become your clients. An everyday example is a high street painting shop, they will often have the words trade paint somewhere visible in or on their window or signage, it is to attract the trade. Everyone else, if they notice it, will simply think, ok, this shop sells paint for the trade, it is probably good. So, the term shouts to the trade who see trade discounts and it still speaks to average consumers where it shows potential for professionalism if they see anything at all.

In C, we talk about achievements

This is the result, the things that your customers typically want to achieve. Let's say it is Springtime, it's getting warmer outside and now is the time to treat the woodwork of our property, C could protect your woodwork, or something like that.

In D, we introduce what to avoid

This is the beginning of a one-two punch, a popular boxing technique, the idea is to give them not one but two compelling reasons, this is a placeholder that could hold more than one thing to avoid. For example: water damage and subsequent shrinkage.

In E, we introduce what may be desired

In this way, we end the template positively, on a high note, maybe one item, maybe two. For example, ensure year-round protection that looks good too.

We can use the same template to target different people, different products and services, different times of year, in so many places, even on-line and as a template for email messaging too. You can use this all year round and by changing the elements A, B, C, D & E. You will always appear to have the most up-to-date and relevant messages.

Don't forget the love!

Message to market match is key, and if possible, we should try and throw a little bit of love in them, which is done, by the way, automatically in the form of recognition of who we are targeting. There is nothing to stop us from giving it even more.

Chapter 4: How business owners can find golden opportunities using just one word

From the beginning of search, sometime in the mid-90s, keywords became available to us. It has always been possible to discover them in website log files and they used to be shared by search engines, although they are increasingly hidden nowadays. Oddly, it is as if search engines want to hide their results. However, there are two places that offer immense insights, and they lie in the auto populated search boxes, for instance, on Google.com and Amazon.com.

Google shows a general search intent, which is useful, while Amazon shows buyers' intent, which could be critical. It all depends on whether what you sell can be sold on Amazon. If you are trying for thought leadership, then Google may give you more clues, if you are trying for product sales, Amazon may be the one for you.

Either way, with a clear understanding of contextual intent, you can readily give your on-line searcher, reader, or buyer a steer towards you by publishing popular content on the web. Popular content is more than just SEO. Popular content is where you can drive readers and readers enjoy and practically engage. You may have heard the search engine bots can detect all this activity through the application of cookies and so on. Whatever systems they have that work, the point is that if the content is useful and engaging, your business will benefit from the obvious attribute of either achieving sign up or sales. Where being search engine friendly is a happy spin off, if it happens, to drive traffic.

Nowadays, the spin-off of getting traffic from search only occurs for sure if you pay for the traffic and only if you sell something can this provide a return on investment. Bear in mind, many businesses employ pay per click without making any sales who may as well be giving their money directly to Google. In any case, pay per click largely amounts to a pyramid scheme. If you think about, there can only be one or two at the top and they pay through the nose.

Increasingly, this is happening in social media, for instance, Pinterest and Facebook, where the only real way to get traffic is to pay for it. The cost of traffic is admittedly less expensive.

There are, however, a few big sites where the cost of traffic is minimal to nothing, like Twitter, reddit, and Quora. They have millions of not just visitors but engaged users, just the type you want and usefully segmented user groups too, so you can easily tap into them and say hi. Anyway, the point is to create an on-line destination that is genuinely engaging and maybe makes sales too. These tend to occur when you have good stories in place that people follow and play with. Literally, you want to provide an experience, as that is what your users expect and demand. For privileged, or additional programmed access, some of those will pay for it too. They do it in their millions, look at Disney+ for instance, a subscription product, 100% story.

All markets are saturated. Aren't they?

If you were looking for a book you would, naturally enough, start with the keyword: perhaps a business keyword. It is likely your topic area for books is saturated, crowded out, there are thousands of books, with little chance, no opportunity, and no hope. Or, at first, you may think. However, when you look closely, and type your search words slowly, Amazon auto-populates the search for you.

You may have seen it, if not, go to Amazon and search for something and see if any words you did not type are suggested, usually, there are some. This indicates what many others have searched for, and as it is a common search, Amazon helps you to save some time and pushes you in the direction you may well have gone anyway, by steering you with a suggestion. In turn, this can lead to a selection of products and books.

All Amazon users have the intent and means to buy

It is worth noting that Amazon is the world's best product-led search engine. Everyone who uses it has both the intention and the ability to buy. This sets it apart from Google, where many people search as they happen to be looking for information, jokes, or porn.

Anyway, I quickly realized it would make sense for my book to target the term 'How to start a business'. I found an opportunity. At that time, there were few books on the subject and the quality of the competition, to my eyes, seemed poor. To quickly come to the point, I wrote the book, published it, and now, on Amazon, you can find my book listed against that search term. I sell multiple copies every day, and they usually lead the search results. My book is the most popular. Not of all books, just for the search terms targeted.

First, we start with the question of what search term to use. Second, we focus on the specific search term found. Third, hedge your bets somewhat and include the search term in the name of your book.

Results!

Depending on which day and time you look, invariably, my book is in the number one position for that search term and on many other page ones. Being indexed well and appearing in lots of search results means I sell a few copies of my book on most days of the week. It is not super big bucks, but hey it all adds up and I am extremely pleased to have readers and to get their feedback, most of them seem to love my work.

I also ensured the keyword appears in the writing of the book and is clearly the subject of the book. This means as Amazon indexes my book, they find the content matches as the keyword is frequently used internally, within the copy of the book too. Starting a business is an activity I have helped thousands to do over the years for real.

I also made sure the keywords were used in the book blurb (the back cover of the book and the book description on the Amazon site) and I wrote a press release about the launch of the book. I still send press releases to newspapers, magazines, and websites around the world as I promote the book. No sensible journalist would ever publish a review without a press release. A very good journalist I know told me and I hit my head with the palm of my hand when I heard it, as it was so obvious, yet at the time I did not realize. You see, I am still learning! You can teach old dogs' new tricks.

Yes, you guessed right, the press release included the keyword too. The whole idea of the press release is to save the journalist the time needed to read the book. Busy journalists tend to paraphrase or, in some cases, copy your press release directly and publish it as they are entitled to do. This means the chances are high for content relating to your book to appear as you have written and with a link to your Amazon sales page, with keywords in the copy. Links of this nature, from credible authority sites, increase the likelihood your book will hit the number one spot and may assist your readers in finding your book through Google too.

Why does this work?

Hopefully, it stands to reason that by targeting a given keyword, you can find an opportunity and use it as the basis to write a personal story and share some experience, with the express intent of helping readers looking for help in starting a business of their own. The name of the book, cover, blurb, press release and content itself are all focused on keywords.

You can do the same. You don't need to write a book. Whether you are planning a book, a podcast, or an article or are looking for a story to write that is popular. You may just be looking for ideas. Using the technique, I just described, you will find the most popular. You will find books on the topics you can review and see what topics they cover and discover more ideas. Also, you may want to read the reviews, particularly the bad reviews. You want to see what readers complain about and see if you can address their complaints. This is another great way of coming up with content related to your business, where you know there is friction you can solve.

The bottom line is that keywords are proven to resonate with readers, as we can see so many readers searching for them. We refer, of course, to the phrases suggested in the search bar. Look at the auto-complete options very carefully, they contain hidden gems.

Chapter 5: Got a story to tell an audience?

This is the easiest storytelling framework you will ever find.

It was as if this framework was designed for business storytelling as there are just five parts, two of which you should already have: you know who your customers are likely to be, and you know what you want to promote. Those two parts happen to inform us with the application of A, B, some of D, some of C and E.

Where A stands for Action, B for Background, then Development, Climax, and Ending.

Where [A] is the typical actions taken by your customers. [B] could be their background. [D] could concern something of importance to them, perhaps relevant at this time of year, and [C] the climax of the story is the transition your product or service bring about. [E] is the opportunity to sum and conclude the moral of the story, which no doubt would be we are glad we became a customer of yours.

Novelist Alice Adams, 14.8.1926 – 27.5.1999 sometimes followed a pattern she called ABCDE. It provides the basis for outlining a short story she once described to a friend in her favorite city, San Francisco. The outline has been marveled over, tested to the limit, and shared ever since. It so happens this simple structure lends itself to short stories and web writing and it encourages a quick rate of reveal too.

Open your story with [A] an Action.

For instance: In 2012, while visiting San Francisco, I took the opportunity to take an Alice Adams tour.

In [B], background, we explain what happened.

It turns out the bus that we thought we were going to take was a multi-colored camper van, just big enough to squeeze my wife, my two sons and mother in the back. I was offered a front seat with the tour operator, guide and, as it turned out the driver and owner of said camper van. So far, it was a typical San Francisco day. Fair, not quite what you wanted, but somehow brighter and better!

[Still B] We felt slightly let down, bemused and delighted, all at once. Not exactly the bus we imagined, yet, we were about to have a very personal service, or so we thought.

56

[D] time to expand and develop our feelings.

Although I had a great, wide, and panoramic view with lots of foot space up front, the same could not be said of those in the back. There were large windows but to the left and right, neither ahead or rearward, unless they were seated close to one of the two ends, so their views were obviously not so satisfactory.

When we arrived downtown at the Fish market, the rest of the family really wanted to take the time to look around and get the feel of the place. The only feeling they had got was the smooth tarmac through the suspension, which was not terrible. However, we were on vacation, and they expected a decent view.

So, as you can imagine, words were voiced about who might be sitting up front for the next leg of our journey. It was quite clear it would not be me again.

You can see how the story might develop and, for the moment, the story will continue to develop [D] as we found the opportunity to include the elements that coincided to cause a change. A change in mood, a change in circumstances, from peace to concern, and so we come to [C]:

Everything changed after that.

[C] Describe the transformation

State how things were before the transformation, how the transformation was completed or how it occurred, and what happened as a result?

[E] Explain to the reader why this story matters.

Why was it useful to share? This is where we make the point, perhaps declare the moral of the story. How can the reader apply the learning to their own life, what could they add? Or make sure they avoid?

Most importantly, make heroes of your customers

As you may surmise, you can start this story with the end in mind [E] and [A], the action could include the normal actions of your target market. Without a good story, you would be selling mundane sheds to locals.

With the story [A] … [E] you should try to make a local family the heroes of the story and your shed could be the very shed that saves the day. The objective is to leave the readers emotionally connected to the shed as it is for the good of the family and afford extra protection.

Your story would contrive to show your shed protecting everyone against bad weather and fostering warm relationships. While the transformation might be a missing back door key (a simple non harmful problem) arrives back with the mom who popped to shop. While she was gone, a freak storm bucketed down, the back door had automatically locked itself and the only place available for protection was the recently purchased shed – to the rescue!

Or something like that.

Whatever your story and the constituents involved, knowing some of the key players makes the writing of the story much easier. This is almost a paint by numbers story framework that is both loose and highly adaptable. Making the writing of a story a breeze. All good for web readers, fast to complete to.

Story length – it's your choice!

Obviously, you can make your story as long or as short as you wish. Also, with this kind of delineation it is also possible to put in subheads, or as and when you can see short one-liners in use, these can be emboldened to break up the story and act as visual subheads too. Just be careful to write the sub heads so the story can be appreciated rapidly as many will read the sub heads first, then, and increasingly, for many, only then will they go back and read the full story. The words of the story should be written using language a junior grade could read and understand. Ideally, your prose should be as spoken words, rather than conform to formal grammar.

Here is a much shorter example (starting with where the action is):

[A] In 2010 I noticed [B] banner advertising had evolved into a wide range of shapes and sizes which meant [D] ad campaigns were difficult to manage and so I concluded as chair, [C] it was time to set a standard, and [E] that standard still exists today.

Chapter 6: The 4 base appeals of business storytelling

The Hierarchy Of Needs is not a scientifically proven formula, although it is widely accepted as being an extremely important theory that describes and, in a few ways, defines what motivates us.

Many of us will understand how important it is to not just tell, but to sell. The difference is that telling is like an instruction, an order, taken to the extreme by putting a gun to your head. Whereas selling requires us to make information available and for listening to choose to accept it and act accordingly if they want to. Personally, I always prefer voluntary to forced actions.

On the one hand, you may need to hold the authority of a gun to require someone to act, while on the other requires the authority of persuasion. When it comes to the Hierarchy Of Needs, a gun directly threatens the element of Endurance, also referred to as self-preservation, it is a simple if not brutal equation, as in, money or your life. As brutal as it is, it is a technique still employed today by despotic pariahs around the world. We shall leave the forcing decision as a denied route we would not support.

Instead, we will look in great depth into how we might make information available and why a listener may choose to listen. This way, the listener can follow through with enthusiasm and an emotionally less exhaustive process that leaves the door open to further conversations, listening and ultimately conversion.

Being the best in sales

Having sold, worked in a professional sales environment, I have worked with many salespeople and their customers, and I find the levels of friendship forged remarkable, and often surprisingly long lasting. As you can imagine, an initial meeting of two people, a buyer and seller, may well occur for transactional purposes. Yet time and time again, sales are not made because customers must buy, sales are made for a combination of logical and emotional reasons.

I have attended a multi-day sales training event where the entire focus has been on the number of decisions a prospective customer has to make and there are typically just a few that are logical, the rest being entirely emotional and about the fit between the perception of what the buyer wants and what the supplier can provide and most of the decisions, which may affect a long time in the future are entirely based on what happens exclusively during the sales process.

Like all good stories, sales start at the beginning

A salesperson will invariably start with an open question such as "Nice to meet you, how are you?" The opening question may relate to the weather, the location, the person who made the introduction or it may even start with something we can all agree on, such as it is nice to meet at last.

However the conversation starts, the salesperson will ask an open question as the objective for the salesperson is to learn what concerns you. Sales invariably occur problem solving and these in turn often match to the Hierarchy Of Needs..

The Hierarchy Of Needs

These are the common needs of most people, ordered by the acronym WARE, provided to help you memorize them:

1. Wealth (Money)
2. Affection (Romance)
3. Respect (recognition)
4. Endurance (self-preservation)

For Wealth, you must show Affection to gain Respect with which you should Endure.

Wealth (Money)

Wealth is possibly not the most important thing on the list, it has its pride of place as number one on the list, as after all, the purpose of a business is to generate wealth.

Money is a motivator, and it is measurable.

Most of us commit actions to effect gain. Wealth gains may be intellectual, time, or financial. Sometimes time or knowledge can be considered more valuable than money, as money is usually a short-term gain, here today, gone tomorrow. Whereas knowledge, once you have it, you can use it and you still have it to use again. On the other hand, time is something we only have once and once used, it is gone forever.

The mistakes of many enterprises is to focus exclusively on money

Not only will they miss all the other opportunities to acquire wealth and become successful, but they also often force themselves to work harder to earn less. Focusing on money alone often brings people to discount their services to be cheaper than the rest and this can mean more sales, more customers, more wear and tear, more costs, and lower margins.

If you are positioned as a premium player with higher prices, your ability to resolve problems, make inventions and lead the field is much enhanced as you need to sell less to make more. Ultimately, this can lead to enhanced reputation, higher profits, more repeated business, and a more satisfactory outcome where price is less relevant to quality or timing.

Affection (Romance)

Romance can go too far. To put it crudely, if you were looking at a news website and there were four stories on the front page, the one that had the words 'nude protester' in the headline with a picture would most likely get the most views and the first clicks.

You might not be surprised to learn how commonly this technique is used by certain well-known daily papers who are simply in the business of gaining attraction. Recently, a protester was nude apart from a small g-string. Photographs of the person in question featured on numerous websites and no-doubt did a lot for the cause, not to mention the policeman who had to 'look after' the situation.

This is an example of how it is possible to break the preoccupation of your readers' minds and it could work for one of several reasons, from disgust to delight. I can't believe someone would do this! To "I can't get enough of this!", and: "are there more pictures?". It is romance as opposed to sex, as nothing sexual has happened.

Romance is invariably all about future promise and is often entertaining or humorous. Future promise is commonly employed to romance a customer or partner to do something now in return for the promise of a future experience or expectation. If I buy it from you (now), you will deliver it to me (in the future).

In advertising, you may be promised to be seen by more people, your reputation could build and, if you make a good offer, results will be measurable. You will meet genuinely new customers. Damage limitation is mitigated with the phrase: Of course, there can be no guarantees.

Respect (Recognition)

Most people lust after recognition, there are many reasons.

Recognition can raise importance and equate to higher income, a better job, or simply a better standing in society. Many of us are competitive and being recognized helps us to be seen as being one of the winners. This is particularly the case for the more sociopathic.

There are many today who put more in store with respect to what others think about them, than what they deliver. This is not to say everyone who clamors for recognition is a sociopath, simply they do exist. A sociopath is at the extreme end of the spectrum. Most people are not extreme in their demands for respect or for recognition, most people would simply expect it as a matter of course, due to their longevity in a role or because their role should command a certain, or minimum amount of respect.

It is polite to be respectful, too. There are many who do not need it, indeed many who are surprised by it, yet enjoy recognition when it occurs. It is easy to give, so why not give it?

Taken a step further, many businesses design awards programs, for instance, where the objective is to put their target clients on a pedestal.

I was responsible for launching the Ernst & Young Entrepreneur of The Year Awards program which, some 25 years later, is now a global phenomenon. The awards industry is a big, prestigious event that occurs globally and, in some cases, the Oscars, for instance, are televised.

Scale is not an issue. The bigger the better, sure, yet the point is recognition and if you can run, organize, or sponsor an event of this type, it can be a very powerful communications tool. The Trojan Horse story of annual award events is to share your reason why story as part of the event promotional activity before, during and after each event, each year.

We all know that Rome was not built in a day. Although I was not on that job.

We expect things to take time. We will imagine business can be completed quickly and we can process many orders, yet, sadly, as most of us discover most of the time, what we want to happen does not always happen at the speed we expect. So, we endure.

We take one step at a time. We discover some aspects of what we do get to be completed quickly and other things take longer. Sometimes for random reasons, sometimes we employ complex processes where time is a component. For instance, if we are in manufacturing, we may have to wait for the glue to set. In business, it can often take a while for trust to build.

On the other hand, some of our clients may not give us all their business as they want to make sure they have more than one supplier. Indeed, we may want to source our supplies from more than one supplier for self-preservation reasons too.

There are many ways we engage with others, and they are likely to engage with us where the primary motive is, indeed, self-preservation. This may be the reason for the delay or why our sales objective takes longer to achieve than necessary. We either must endure the wait, or we deliberately manage our environment so we will endure. These are issues and potential benefits we should look for in our customer stories and share our own stories to let others know we are aware of and will support them in their mission for endurance.

One of the methods many enterprises use to demonstrate endurance is their adherence to quality, safety, human and cyber standards. Many seek third-party endorsement through the process of certification, and accreditation where the benefit is not simply to share their story, usually they end up with a more secure, certain, and reliable business too.

Enterprise certification is not random. Certification, for instance, is usually done for a specific reason, to trade with another specific organization such as government, medical or military clients who demand their suppliers work to certain standards and these are best certificated.

Certification is a story that lends itself to being told. Clients may be surprisingly interested, especially if they meet with the story of who they are, especially if they also serve the medical, government or military markets, which in many cases represent a significant proportion of the available markets. Thus, accreditation can help to convey trust, and may well meet a minimum criterion to allow another enterprise to buy from you.

Your story is about building the future

When you consider the story from these four perspectives, you will find more ways to build out your story and to communicate the benefits. In addition, your understanding of others, potential clients, suppliers, and partners will improve when you consider them from these perspectives.

Chapter 7: Use your stories twice

All businesses could use the power of story more.

There are many who talk about the power of story as being an enabler so a business and its brand may be loved. A powerful outcome.

The more people love your business, the stronger the brand, although being loved by everyone does not suit every enterprise. For many, it is vital only to be loved within their inner world, their niche. This is often the outcome authority figures look for.

Many businesses miss out on employing powerful stories, as they feel they are fiction. Yet stories can be employed and remain private, off the radar, which would suit some.

The story itself is not one thing. The story is not just about being loved.

There are many stories you can tell. When it comes to business-related stories, they typically fit into one of two main groups, internal and external.

Typical medium-sized and larger business stories

Most have a big focus on internal stories. Many will have a mission to tell more external stories, yet, for many reasons, rarely seem to get around to it. There is always a new project.

Typical small business stories

If they employ a story at all, small businesses generally have one story that often centers on the ambition and objectives of the CEO, focused on growth. There are always more clients to win.

Focus first on telling a core story effectively

There are many types of stories large and small businesses can employ. If you focus first on telling your core story, your founder story, the one which is about why you do what you do. This is the foundation of all your core stories. One story that you will build upon. Or looked at differently, if you feel you need to tell a story and you want it to be new, then tell your original story in a new way.

The chances are you will confidently tell the story. The chances are all those who have heard it before, will feel reassured with your reaffirmation of who you are and what you stand for.

The more you tell your founder story, in more ways, the more powerful the story becomes, and your enterprise will become more effective, faster. There is no need to be diverted by new stories if you have already had a core story to tell. The first consideration is how a new story relates to those you already tell?

Internal stories

All enterprises have internal, operational stories, even small companies. Most businesses are likely to have to keep some data secure and this security feature could be supported through story as a definite, not to be ignored, natural, essential part of operations. We should know what data we collect, what we do with it, how long we keep it, why it is necessary and how long to keep it. Great story elements!

As data is held securely, then access can be monitored, and results (or lack of) can be communicated with everyone, highlighting the fact they need to review and potentially sign off information as being received. This information can feed into management reporting, so further action (stories) can be decided upon, such as new and different strategies to ensure compliance is undertaken and security and privacy features maintained.

It is easier to manage process through story. Although traditional elements, such as recording and stipulating precise processes should be maintained.

Smaller enterprises are likely to experience fewer internal stories, yet they are still important. For instance, the founder story can be very effective at holding a small business together. Especially when there are just a few key employees. A small company still must work within the law and needs to be wary of cybersecurity. For instance, and is most likely to be damaged if an employee moves on, is poached by a competitor, or sets up in competition.

This can and does happen to larger enterprises, too.

Effective use of strong stories can help thwart a cyber-attack by raising awareness. Similarly, a strong founder, core story can help lock down staff retention and reduce losses through leakage.

The benefit of a story and its power can be measured by what is retained, not necessarily by what is lost. A story can be beneficial without winning anything more. The story is not just about growth; it can also be a protective measure designed and implemented to prevent loss.

External Stories

External stories are employed to great effect by emerging businesses, especially those who seek to upset an industry.

Game changing stories are particularly powerful and can create new industries, even in hitherto mundane sectors. These are often driven by technological change, although I often wonder if the story of AI and Machine Learning is louder than its bite. Does it instill fear within the minds of business owners and managers, or is it used as a ploy by savvy marketers?

There have been many technologies launched by technologists, where the real work was simply outsourced to lower-cost regions of the world, based in opposite time-zones who were able to compete in semi-automated tasks and get the results back to clients quickly. This notably happened in the voice to text-messaging industry in the early days, although over time, it would appear AI and machine learning proved its worth.

There are many businesses born out of the story of potential, literally. These are launched to test the market, to then build a service to match the market's needs. This comes from the lean business methodology where the story of lean describes a Minimum Viable Product (MVP).

The essence of each story can usually be summed up easily. Story power can usually be increased, and the delivery of the story can be widened, usually without breaking a sweat. Simply by telling the story in different ways to suit different times, cultures, markets, locations, the list of variations is almost endless, particularly when combined. Obviously, the more focus we apply, the more explicit, the more exact and the more powerful your story and its impact is to the audience.

How to communicate your story

The story itself is a major component of information delivery. It can be used to position highlights, to encourage consumption, to demonstrate value or use cases and, of course, relevancy.

Important information can be easily uploaded to central systems. This can have several benefits and cost very little. First, your initial messaging can be much lighter and focus more easily on value and relevance and other motivational aspects. This can lead to an organized menu focused on maximizing value and relevance.

There are many staff members who receive notifications of events, and they pay little to no attention to them. Everything seems important, the volume can be unrelenting, in the end, staff organize their own methods to manage the torrent of information.

Staff are likely to say they don't pay attention because there are too many notifications, too little time, and they don't appear relevant. However, they may be important legal requirements.

Classic internal stories are usually to do with internal communications, including acquisitions, integration, legislation, governance, security, tax and financial, results, policy, new regulations, and compliance to name a few. Frequently, these are looked at as someone else's responsibility and ignored.

These can be often unwieldy, too frequent and look like someone is ticking boxes, to make sure the topics are covered for legal reasons, rather than for mission critical reasons, even if they are mission critical.

Unread messaging is sloppy and likely to lead to a slippery slope of more and more being ignored, leading to widespread ineffectiveness and ultimately indifference to the enterprise.

Use packaging to overcome inertia

Information, however dry, still needs to be available to encourage your audience to engage. In addition, when information and data are bundled together intelligently, it can appear to be more useful and less like wading through drying cement.

The way to package information is to put it into context, like the way content is collected in a book, chapter by chapter, when it comes to regularly transmitting and sharing emails, it would be better to put them together as contents of a topical newsletter.

If it was deemed that certain information did not need to be delivered urgently and immediately, then the information could be compiled and similar messages were sent collectively as a digest in one shot, this may make it all more readable and potentially stored as a searchable archive too, perhaps on an intranet, so it is delivered, remains available and may be deployed as a searchable resource. Potentially releasing much more internal value to the organization in the process too.

Communication formats

We all consume information in different ways. Some like to read, some have time to read, especially if they travel long distances, often by train or plane. Others prefer audio, especially if they walk or drive, they can listen while they commute, but they can't take their eyes off the road.

Others like seeing video presentations. A mixture of audio, textual, and other visual clues, including people and things. It depends on what it is you are communicating with and it depends on the needs of your audience too. The more information you can codify as story to suit your audience, the more likely it will be consumed and not missed, lost or wasted.

Chapter 8: Who are you for? How can you compel others to act?

To tell the right story and for our story to be acted upon, we must know more about who we are for.

Customers will tell us what they want and they will move towards their goal.

Who is our audience and how can we help them achieve their goal?

It is down to us to understand our audience and let them know we can help. Yet a lot of us are protective of our story, we may be shy, or overly protective of what we consider to be our business and we do not want to give the game away.

Some of us don't want to brag. When time is short, we might think this is likely to be a big job, and we doubt our ability to write or tell a compelling story. In any case, we have salespeople, or we are salespeople, so let's just sell the darn thing!

I know, I have been to all these places!

The only solution is to start.

Start from the perspective, it is not our story to tell. The stories belong to our audience. We don't necessarily write the story. We could start by recording it. Give yourself a block of time, for example twenty minutes, get started with just an outline, a few bullet points, and then get back on with something you know you will complete, where you know you will do a good job. Treat it all as an experiment and grab twenty-minute chunks of time or more.

Interview your audience

To record a story, we can simply interview our target audience, in this way, we get someone to tell their story. We can learn a lot by lining up a few interviews. We can pick out the important elements of the stories we hear, and we can communicate important points in terms that best suit us both. We should bear in mind that our competitors share our concerns and are also shy or protective.

Increasingly, due to concerns about cybersecurity and the protection of intellectual property and the importance of protecting personally identifiable information, we have created barriers to stop certain levels of communications, and this can get in the way of our ability to tell stories as protection is a deliberate intention. However, communication is still key and, like us, our clients can still share their stories without giving away or providing sensitive information.

Can you feel the force?

The force is our compelling reason to tell the story. We may have to play the sleuth, the investigator. Just like a detective, we want an admission. When we have admission, the story unravels, and we can put the pieces together. It is important to make sense of the story. In police terms, this helps to ensure the right person gets convicted of the crime, as sometimes a person may admit guilt to protect another.

While protecting another is laudable, perhaps honorable, it can get in the way of the truth. If we do not seek the truth, then our story may end up literally misguided, and we will fail in our objectives.

Many business endeavors fail because they tell the wrong story. You can present a case that may be true, yet if your potential client or customer doesn't buy your solution, you will not make progress. There may be a range of good reasons, and the best way to explain them could be through a story. For instance, a case study type of story may demonstrate your solution can process more, go faster, last longer and, on a unit basis, cost less. These are just a few key story attributes you could employ.

Romance The Stone

Clients do not wake up, wanting to be romanced. That is not how romance works. Romance starts simply by showing interest. You must ask questions to understand user stories and then build relationships based on what you discover about them. User story can be a deliberate ploy to romance a potential customer, or, indeed, wider market. You could demonstrate you have already asked thousands within the market about their interest in your product or service, yet today, you would value their opinion to see if the time and cost savings and throughput delivered for others would suit them too.

How to amplify your respect

The more you recognize customers by name and flatter their professionalism or area of expertise, the more they will like you. The more likable you are, the more likely they will reciprocate, stop, take notice, and give you, their time. Respect can be an arresting technique for romance.

There are more values, including liberation and endurance (Dr Maslows Self-preservation) your audience provides, the more material you will collect to talk about in your follow-up communications and potentially provide the basis for a series of campaigns. Each campaign should ideally focus on a single focus or area of appeal, such as the most appropriate (to them) aspects of self-preservation for instance. You only know what is appropriate for your audience if you understand the story of your audience.

Higher values

While your competitors might bang on about features and benefits of their product, if they can focus on anything beyond price, you can beat them on these by simply talking about the important higher values important to your customers.

As you already have customers, and because you have undertaken the research (interviews), we should have already established what customers pay attention to. The story is rarely disguised, and customers are usually found at the core and are part of the fabric of the story. In persuasion, the key is always personal appeal of which much has been written.

The art of asking questions

We approach two-way communication like an investigator where we are looking for admission. When we have our admission, we know, from experience, we will likely hear the rest of their story follow through. Almost as a side benefit, just through listening, we cement our relationships with our customers.

An unfolding story forms the underlying basis for key account management. Sometimes it is as simple as people like to be heard, customers want to know they count, and they expect recognition. Many customers simply object to being sold to, they don't want to hear about you, they want to tell you about themselves. Let them speak.

Story affiliation

When you tell a story, you start to create a reason for an affiliation. For example, supermarkets are large stores with isles of goods. In many cases, in most stores in the same places, with the same goods, the same brands, with some minor differences. However, as their customers, we prefer to shop in certain stores as opposed to others. Some of us shop for price, some of us value the difference, and may prefer to pay slightly more, knowingly, as money is not the issue, quality is. Some of us like the convenience, the manner, the layout, or the location of a given store compared to another.

Yet, each store has an advertising campaign. They each find different ways to sign post their stores. They build consistency so they come across as not simply selling you on stuff, instead you become emotionally committed to them, you develop an affiliation as they communicate their values through stories. When you look at their values through the prism of Dr Maslow's hierarchy of needs, you can acquire insights into how they achieve their objectives.

It's human nature

This is not to complain about stores being sneaky or manipulative, they are, just to demonstrate how much these techniques are in common use at the low value, high volume end of the market as well as the fact that these needs exist at a high level b2b, on a one-to-one basis. In other words, from a human perspective, whether you are in a consumer or business market, the laws of story apply equally, yet the story characters are different, the characters, the price points, the frequency, the location, and the rest are all different.

Story works for mass-markets and on a one-by-one basis

Indeed, it is because it works at an individual level it works at a mass market level, we are all individual thinkers and dreamers who have a view on how the world works and how we would like to live within it. B2b markets are run by people who share the same values. You may believe that professional markets are different.

Crystal clear clarity is a requirement

The difference is that clients look for ever smaller segments, increased specialization. It may be hard to cut through, which means the way you relate to your audience's story had better be crystal clear and telegraphed to them in an obvious way. You must understand your segment with great clarity, so you customers are crystal clear you are for them.

Dog Whistle marketing

Telegraphing to a particular user group is akin to using a dog whistle only a dog can hear. When talking to certain markets, there are certain words, certain turns of phrase that have more meaning and, when seen, can signify you are in the right place. This is how you would communicate, to tell a meaningful story where the reader would most likely act due to your research and understanding of specific market needs.

For instance, when we review small specialist enterprises, we often find they are very uptight about their messaging. Yet when we review those who acquire other businesses in the same industry, they often have an established marketing team who employs traditional marketing methods. This is because they know they are dealing with normal human beings and are beyond being recognized as being part of the "in" crowd and spend more of their time appealing to human needs, such as belonging, affiliation, recognition, respect, self-preservation, wealth, romance, and all or some of the other aspects.

Chances are many big company marketing departments that are not even aware of the techniques they are employing and are just there to fulfill the random wishes of the partners. They may simply be there to respond to diarized industry events that need to be catered for as a matter of sound business practice.

Handling difficult or unknown stories

There are many situations in business where the customer is not and cannot be precisely clear on their objectives. For instance, the objective may be to commission a building, yet the customer is not familiar with the constraints of building regulations.

So, with a brief to invest in a new headquarters building and for the building to be ideally located in a certain place and with an objective to make a statement about the building, or not. The investors will rely on experts to locate the land who will make sure the land is close to the necessary amenities such as power, water, and waste management and meet all the other requirements. A short list of prospects will be drawn up and the investors will make the decision. Success will depend on the interpretation of the story behind the project. This is a common question where the authors of the story cannot clearly articulate what they want. Instead, they have every confidence they will know it when they see it.

When all is done, an approval team made up of other experts will review the recommendations, check the work, and may reject the result, perhaps to allow time for more investigations of any related issues of concern that must be resolved before financial commitment can be finalized.

Similar cycles may occur in the design stage after the land is purchased and the architects are commissioned and so on all the way through to building and eventual fit-out and occupation. These processes can take years to conclude. To shorten the process and achieve the desired outcome, everyone needs crystal clear clarity in the story from the beginning.

Project Management stories

There are defined project management processes known as Prince and Agile, which are fundamentally different in their approach. A key component of both is the objective story. Prince is a waterfall system where one part logically follows from another, the first being a logical beginning, the last step being occupation of a building, or the opening of a bridge for public use, for instance.

Define from the beginning

Prince requires everything to be logically planned out, timed, and costed from the beginning. This is what most investors would want, but it often gets the development stages wrong as it does not know what is involved. Prince works where all the parts are known, for instance, if you build a bridge, you will always select the land first and build from there. You should not start in the air and hope to find land on either side.

The iterative approach

Whereas Agile is an iterative approach and may start anywhere in the story, it does not have to start at a logical beginning or end. Agile is normally employed in areas such as software development, where the first objective is to prove the core technology from which the enterprise will then evolve around it.

For example, the main objective of an agile project is to prove the viability of a project. The initial objective may be to see if we can get one system to talk to another. Based on the data exchanged, we may be able to determine whether it is possible to make decisions and issue commands back to alter the outcome. This might be considered a minimum viable product (MVP) and would be the first deliverable. The point is to prove a story narrative where we have described what we want to do and then, through MVP, to prove it can be done. Once proven, to expand the project to turn an idea into a product or service.

As agile can start in the middle instead of at the logical end of a project, we can get to the heart of the matter quickly, prove the truths needed and the rest can follow through. Most of the agile processes are all about the story of what we want to achieve and for whom. So, knowing the story objectives is critical. Just like writing a story, all we may know when we start is the beginning and end. The objective is to determine exactly what the middle part of the story is.

Fears and frustrations

There are millions of examples of business stories told and shared with team members, many of which will have financial implications and invariably involve a range of people in the process. These are people who will have a wide range of objectives, agendas and, indeed, fears and frustrations. Some will be frustrated with their own projects or agendas being delayed by someone else's agenda. This can lead to dangerous politics, stalemate, checkmates and even destruction if someone is so minded.

Stories, like projects, need to be carefully managed

A project manager does not simply manage the project or the people, there is also the story to manage. In the case of both Prince and Agile, project milestones must be agreed and signed off. This is to demonstrate agreement at a given point in time and helps to create a feeling of joint responsibility. Each is an area of potential friction and frustration.

Why does this matter to business storytelling?

Each small part of the process is a small part of the bigger picture story. It must exist to justify the ongoing life of a project. It is imperative for the project manager to tell the story in terms each participant can understand and reasonably remind each participant of the importance of the current project over other projects.

Storytelling therefore requires a sensitive, knowledgeable approach that can prove difficult to maintain and manage as there is often a wide range of complexities. No matter how frustrations are played out, the project management and other layers of project management need to manage the feelings of all involved to maintain as much good will toward the project despite very difficult circumstances that may arise. Resolutions are largely achieved through communication and agreement with the key story.

Understanding the individual stories of all the players in a large, interconnected project is key as we need to fit the project into the story first and foremost. Then we must relay progress over time to justify how the project story continues to fit and continues to allay fears and frustrations.

Usually, most will voice their objections, fears, and frustrations, although not everyone does. Therefore, detective skills become the imperative, so you can spend time pushing protagonists to reveal their true position, so they work toward resolution while avoiding red-herrings, and other traps to make sure your project is not sidelined, and all the objectives are achieved.

Chapter 9:
5 ways change leads to renewed excitement in your story

As long as the world spins, change occurs, and each spin is an opportunity to renew the interest in your story.

Some things are in our control and at other times, for good reasons and bad, they are not, either way, we need to adjust our story and show how we see it as an opportunity, or as I like to say, as one door slams shut, somewhere in the world, two more open.

On even the darkest of days, we need to search for the upside, and we need to get the news out there to spark ever more interest in our ongoing story. There were many reasons for my first business being called Saga; One was it was quite a story.

1 Introduce change through established lines of communication

Font-line staff and clients share concerns, and they see market changes occur in real-time.

Each is an opportunity to tell our story with renewed vigor in ways to demonstrate how what we do continues to work and how we continue to differentiate. Our story stems from our founders and reaches forward to today and beyond. It is essential to disseminate updates quickly and unambiguously to those front lines, often as a bulletin or as a supplement to an existing newsletter.

For solid communication, the use of printed media can work best, as it does not get buried in an in-box and copies can be left on display at strategic locations, sending strategic messages. We can also hand out and post to potential clients. Controlled communication of important, time-sensitive information can be managed centrally when printed materials are being provided.

The issue for most is speed and so templates could be created and held in stock for short, photocopier or laser printer runs. It can be quite an advantage for top-level information to be disseminated quickly, as speed is of the essence in dealing with either a crisis or opportunity.

Often, only our front-line staff have one-to-one relationships with clients, it is imperative to make life easy for them and to ensure core messages get through.

2: Seek and acknowledge the questions

Sometimes, in the face of events, questions raised are most concerning.

We don't always have the answers, we may, however, know what the questions are most likely to be. It is generally better to acknowledge a change has occurred, a new situation exists, as everyone knows, and our story may well lead us towards finding the answers.

Proactively reacting to change is likely to elevate interest in what we do and position us as part of the solution rather than part of the problem. Often, questions openly shared reveal the competitive advantage of openness and can be employed to invite feedback, as indeed, your front-line staff, clients and customers may well have the answers you are looking for. You can use events to thank them for past contributions and encourage them to work with you to find solutions and answers to the most beguiling questions.

Showing understanding is the route to resolution.

3: Relate change to the founder story

Sometimes, wholesale change drives events, and causes concern.

Few people welcome change and what makes change worse for many is being kept in the dark. Change can cause some to question authority and worry about their own positions. Many businesses undergo change by divesting divisions, terminating old offers, and making new. These stories need to be told sooner rather than later and are best told with reference to our founders' stories to demonstrate straightforward, rational progression. As most have already bought into the founders' story, a change story that references the founders is very reassuring to an existing audience.

Delivering details of changes early and in perspective can help eliminate fears and concerns.

4: Positively pivot into leadership

We have already come so far, and the great news is we can see further ahead.

Change can be good, very good. Innovation often reduces cost, often increases safety, potentially increases speed.

Positive change normally heralds more competitive advantages, demonstrating the ability to both innovate and to pivot in turn to the direction of new opportunity, demonstrating that you can and are most likely to offer more to your customers and clients than anyone else. Thus, change can be a very positive opportunity to demonstrate differentiation and help position your organization as a leader in its field.

Never hesitate to take the opportunity to step up and step forward.

5: Negative change for managing decline

Managed decline avoids disaster and aids transition

All enterprises operate according to the well-honed bell curve of business, the rise, leveling out followed by decline. There are difficulties at every stage, none of which are easy. Problems occur when decline is not managed effectively, especially if they are buried or hidden.

The right attitude would be to use decline as an opportunity to pivot into a different business area of growth. Sometimes declines are seasonal and par for the course, nothing to worry about. The bottom line is, if the market does not want it, you can't sell it.

The solution to decline is often the relaunch, which, as always, requires the retelling of your story coupled with reasons why your new offer is good. A good story is often the only thing that will make a difference. Stories wane just as products do, however, all we need to do is to tell the founders' story with a new twist to reflect the current state of the market, or better, the world.

The story we in effect tell is we were right then, as we are today with a new current twist. However, we don't tend to admit the relaunch is due to a slump in sales. Instead, we search for a positive reason to introduce a launch, the classic is 'new and improved'!

Chances are the change you face will be different.

However, the chances that these outlined may spark a thought. Or perhaps you are able to take some of the solutions as part of a cross pollination process to help you to devise a solution to resolve the changes you face.

Chapter 10:
3 ways to connect more without losing the plot

When it comes to benefits, there are emotional and other feelings our customers have, about us, or the product we supply, in terms of what it does for them. The more we tap into their story, the more we will sell.

1 Who are you really aiming at?

Are we selling a product or a service? Are we helping our customers remember or recreate happy memories they once had? Are they able to do more with their children, their family, or their community? The more you can create the social scene, reunite them with their friends and family, the better.

This is more than just selling a product or service; this is the ability to revive and recreate those special moments. It is important to enable a continuation of the social glue that holds us all together and provides us so much more value in terms of memory and future dreams of the way we were and the way we could be with others. This is the reason why many things are bought beyond basic utility. We don't buy simple things because we need to fulfill a practical objective, we buy because of how it will enable us to meet our family and friends and enjoy our lives.

If this was not the case, we would still be buying the Ford Model A in black.

As customer service agents, as suppliers, we need to understand our customers beyond the utility, display our products and offer our services in the context of who our customers are hoping and expecting to spend their lives with. We need to show them the opportunities extended and allow them to picture who they are aiming at, perhaps by including pictures of groups of people nearby, with, or on whatever is being sold. Then, the benefit of the benefit is more than one dimensional. What is the second realistic, true north dimension behind what is being sold and bought? How can you bring that into the picture and assist the discussion? How can you help your customers invoke those memories so they can feel the emotion of what it is like to be an owner? How will they feel again when those scenes come to life and are relived?

The more you know about who, why and what the more you can invoke those thoughts and memories.

Often, when it comes to emotions and feelings, we are taken to a place and a time of pleasant happiness and enjoyment. A time of warmth by the fire, places where we have experienced the inner warmth and glow of camaraderie.

As humans, we are social animals, we enjoy trust and friendship with others and in sales, we want to create those exact same feelings to close a sale.

Therefore, we want to do all we can to recreate the scene. We can do this through staging and set dressing, we can also achieve this through discussion. In sales, we should not limit ourselves to a mere description of a product or service, its' dimensions, scale, and scope, instead, as well, we should invoke thoughts and memories about the application and how in its future location it is likely to resonate with your loved ones, visitors, friends and perhaps your customers. We want to show how each can take value from being reminded of certain feelings and warm emotions derived from the sounds, the temperature and location of where the product or service is to be employed and how and when it is likely to be of impact.

The more we help and support these thoughts, feelings, and emotions, the more we can take our potential customers closer to the place in their past and help to ensure their future is as good if not better. Or, in their mind's eye, the more we find ways to resonate with and support our customers, make a good decision, and select the right solution that most ideally fits their wants, needs, emotions and feelings.

3 Make it personal

Sales are not just about making the sale. Sales are about fitting into the life of your buyer. You need to understand who you are selling to and there are certain things you are expected to ask, for instance where someone hails from and where the product or service is likely to be used or employed. You can ask about the buyers' intentions and timescales, all normal, standard, everyday questions, some of which you may be able to surmise, for instance, if someone is waiting to buy, it is easier to be certain they are ready to buy now.

However, the questions you ask don't just help you select the most ideal product or service to suit them, they also enable you to recreate the scene they are trying to recreate. The closer you can get to that for them, the more likely you will make the sale.

In recreating a family scene, we want to see if we can call on all of our senses, perhaps the smell of the kitchen, the touch of a small child's hand in ours, the warmth of the sun on our skin, our feelings of being alive and our pride and emotions related to those present.

We can make things glow in the minds of our buyers and we can usually tell from their reaction whether we are headed in the right direction and course correct as we go, we want to minimize jarring. You can summarize, recap, and ask them what else they imagine might complete the picture, not necessarily as a leading sales question, but to complete the picture, where what you are selling sits neatly in the middle. The elements will vary, yet overall, you are trying to set a scene that is personal to them, and, in turn, this makes it personal to you too. Your buyer wants to do business with you, simply because you understand what they want to achieve.

As the scene creator, you put yourself in a position of importance and authority. Better still, if you can change the background, such as music, lighting, seating, and so on, you can give your potential customers a drink and make sure they feel welcomed and warm, these are all scene changes you can make. The objective is to make their buying event as personal as possible, most of these things cost little, and the time spent will vary according to the value of the packages you plan to sell.

Chapter 11:
The referral
story

I want to write a
book on referrals,
and I may yet.

It is such an important topic it would be remiss not to include a chapter on referrals.

Most businesses startup with referrals.

Initial business is usually struck with people we know through personal relationships, often locally. After a while, after the business is proven and is hungry for more customers, business owners and managers start to look further afield and may attend network events, trade shows and potentially advertise.

At trade shows it is expected to have giveaways and information to pass on. This is a big industry, and the usual pattern is to hand out branded notepads, pens, bookmarks, window ice scrapers and so on. There are a million plastic doodads you can buy. I have had squeeze balls made up. It does engender basic feelings of friendship and open conversations. There is nothing like handing out gifts. It is basic, elementary bribery. Somewhere, someday the giveaways may trigger an all-important new business call, maybe, potentially. It works, it has worked for me, it is unreliable though and it does not differentiate your business from all the other exhibitors who also give stuff away.

Give away information, not things

Some business owners up the ante by increasing the value and therefore the potential worth of the giveaway and that is not a bad strategy, it can create buzz. I like the idea of offering more value and probably the best way to deliver value is to offer information to really help solve problems.

The first time I noticed the power of this was when I printed a how to guide, which was a ten-step success booklet that showed what other businesses needed to do to get to the top of search engines. This was in the early days of search before you could just pay your way to the top.

Provide advisory information

First, it is useful to show people they can achieve an objective. These are the kind of people who will step forward, grab a copy, and potentially engage in a conversation. From the stand, or at a networking event, you offer it and ask why, about their interest, their business and why it is worth their while to get to the top. A conversation starter. Your information implies you are an expert. You have so much knowledge of the subject that you are willing to give away some of what you know to help others. This is a great impression to make, especially as it is founded on the truth. It shows your passion for the subject, too.

Secondly, the document answers the kind of questions most new clients ask about. For example, how do you work, what are the next steps? You can gloss over how you work to some extent, after all, you don't want to bore people with all the technical detail, and you can give a high level and even an entertaining answer. The important parts are the next steps, this is what we want our potential customers to focus on and we want to make it easy and reward for them to do so.

A surprising comment I hear often at exhibition-type events is that visitors come on behalf of others, a relative or their team. They will explain that they are not directly interested in themselves, or necessarily likely to buy, they know someone in their team is interested and they are collecting information for them. So, there you are, you heard it directly from the audience, they want information not logos on plastic and while they will all accept the plastic, it does not convey much apart from the fact you are there and if they are indeed handed over, then you may get a website visit. If your give away is too nice, it just might not ever get handed over.

Create a stampede!

Another opportunity was when I was at a startup rally and as a sponsor, I was given the microphone for just minutes as part of the sponsorship package to explain how I could help the audience. In the two minutes allotted I explained I had 100 copies of 'How To Earn More Money Through Networking' with me, it was a new guide I had written just for this event and I am sorry, I don't think I had brought enough for the 200 delegates here, so they are available right now, on a first come, first serve basis.

A queue had formed before I had finished speaking and a moment later, a stampede effect was created as the whole audience left their seats and formed a crowd around my stand as each was desperate to get their own copy.

I handed them out in exchange for email addresses, as I explained, I also had a part two which had not arrived from the printers. I would like to send part two by email. That was my story. The fact was I had not written it yet. It had not been sent to the printers, so it was true it had not come back either. I wrote part two that night, edited it in the morning and sent out pdf copies early in the afternoon. I also invited recipients to fill in an on-line form to send them a printed copy of both parts by post. About half gave me their addresses. This in turn allowed me to write personal letters to them and created more good will. This resulted in a very worthwhile amount of business which far exceeded the cost of event sponsorship.

Start a paid members' site

One thing the information I handed out did was drive people toward my membership website where they could acquire more information, and this then enabled me to tell them about the paid membership program that was on offer and how they could find further assistance and support. A small percentage signed up, which was how my first membership site started.

Membership was modest at first, and it grew over time. Therefore, I realized the need to create more information. Here I wanted to create information members could pass along and this was where I really started to develop a story, as I wanted to tell the story about why I was sending information by post and not just sending pdfs by email. Well, there were two reasons. The first is, as you probably know, not everyone opens all emails. Even when your email contains good stuff, important information, if your email is not opened whether it is skipped or missed, the information might as well have not been produced for all the value it is going to deliver.

However, if you send information by post, your recipient is much more likely to receive it, open it and know they got it. There's one more thing. A piece of paper, or booklet is often stored and has the additional merit of being reviewed in the future and paper can be passed on, shared, filed, and reviewed again later. Good information just keeps on giving!

The sharing of information is key

I highly recommend you send your best information by post and by PDF. It is, on the one hand, annoying when members' only information gets out there, on the other hand, it is a huge compliment and can often wind up with the recipient deciding it is so good, or looking at your sign-up offer and deciding it is so good they decide they want all in. They want to be members of equal standing to their colleagues, who may be, in effect, be saying, let's do this together and collaborate as a team. This is a compelling pitch and, as the membership program manager is great to facilitate, if we can get people to work together in groups, chances are they will support each other and grow together and, to an extent, try to outdo each other, to be the more invested.

I used to think of this as affiliated marketing, until affiliate marketing became a thing about 15 years ago. I have given it a new name now, which I hope shall stick - cohort marketing. We shall see.

How your good story can 'force' people to spend more!

It all starts by showing people how they can avoid classic beginner's mistakes and focus on the areas that count. You can work on this to make it so the only supplier they could hire is you, too.

There are several benefits. First, charging a fee identifies those who are most seriously interested in.

Secondly, the fees cover the costs of marketing and, personally, I just love self-liquidating marketing programs. These are marketing processes that spread the word and pay for themselves, and leave the door open for further sales opportunities.

This is the third point, including a membership program that can unlock a hidden income stream which in turn locks the commitment to you early on. For instance, there is no reason you could not allow 100% of the membership fees as a discount on something bigger they may want to invest in.

Creating a burning hole in the pocket syndrome 'forces' people to spend more money on you.

The burning hole in pocket syndrome

In the sales pitch for membership, one of the benefits of membership can easily include membership only discounts.

Discounted attendance tickets for future events, special members' only prices for services, and, of course, members can be the first to see and try new offers from you.

The way to make this work is always to make an offer with a deadline. This adds a timeline to your offer and makes every offer a limited-time event. These are attractive to people, and they trigger scarcity, one of the key sales triggers, according to Joseph Sugarman, who I had the pleasure of meeting and who wrote the book: Triggers.

Most will agree, this is a better story than just handing out nicknacks and freebies.

At your next event, why not try both? Also, when you have good material and there are no events, which has been the case, due to Covid, there's nothing to stop you from making the offer of free guidance through email, advertising, and on-line events to propagate your story.

100

After Referrals, what next?

For most businesses, nothing! Although they start with referrals, few have any kind of ongoing system to facilitate further referrals. This is odd, when you think this is the most common way for businesses to start up. Plus, as so many businesses don't like to pay for salespeople or have any marketing. Instead, the main strategy of many is to rely on hope. A common alternative you can see often is spraying and praying. Like the hope strategy, a business will flood (or spray) a marketplace with an offer, normally one led by price and then pray someone takes them up on the offer. You don't often see these campaigns repeated, so you know they don't work.

The better method, if you must spray and pray, is to offer information. Granted, it is more involved, long-winded even, but it reduces the friction for enquirers. It also helps you to focus resources on people who ask for assistance, so you should see conversion rates increase.

Instead of asking people to buy now, you ask instead if they would like more information. As a result, you may discover more about what they want to buy, what they could buy and perhaps when they will buy. This information will give you more prospect opportunities and help you convert more buyers and, shore up a sales pipeline, provide confidence for your own future and demonstrate better response numbers.

All of this is dedicated to your opening story, the story about how you can steer potential clients towards success. There are many more stories and for this, the first thing I do is invite people to become members of a separate free membership website from where I can give them more information and more support, invite them to on-line meetings and so on.

The purpose is simply to get to know the audience and for members of the audience to get to know you. To build trust. To take a position of authority in their interest and to help them where you can. There are many new stories you can share with members.

One of those stories is why they should become a paid member and how later, if appropriate, they can get their whole investment back, either through the value of information already shared, or by setting their investment against a future bigger purchase, preferably, both.

Part 2: On Writing

Chapter 12: Why write stories?

The truth is most of us write stories for one of three main reasons. To get our opinion out there, so our voice is heard. To demonstrate to others (like our peers and parents) we can make a difference or simply because we believe everyone has a book inside us and we do too. However, there is another big reason to write a story and that is to help people engage with your enterprise.

We are all tuned to story, all humans are born surrounded by stories. We respect a good story and have done since a young age and so we all turn to listen to a good story. A story has a way of cutting through and can provide focus, understanding, comprehension and can drive people to take action.

From a business perspective, the story serves a single purpose: to help interested people become customers.

I think we can all recall times when we planned to buy something yet decided not to when we were diverted or asked for too much information when all we wanted to do was buy. So, what did we do? We bought it from someone who made it easier.

If we either have no story to follow or the story is simply wrong, then so will be the customer journey. One way to check is to see if there is any story associated with the existing customer journey and to do this, we need to map the journey.

Customer journey mapping is vital because many customer journeys are either inappropriate or indirect. It is bad enough to be indirect but lacks appropriateness. It is as if some businesses try to put clients off. This happens when someone is determined to add a step to the customer buying process. This may be because of legislation, compliance, or regimented systems with too little flexibility, or which are misunderstood.

You often hear of clients who battle through your systems, determined to make a purchase. The reason they do is because they find your story so compelling, they are prepared to go to battle with your systems to win through in the end. You must ask yourself if this is good for business? The kind of thing you would encourage. What you learn is there are those who have not considered the client's journey, let alone mapped it out.

The problem with, and how to harness social media

Most people stand for things and make statements, and these are seen posted across social media all the time. Unfortunately for most, a statement is made and there is no follow through. One reason why social media is so short-lived, living seemingly for just nanoseconds, and transitory.

However, statements work as they are usually the basis of engagement, headline, lead, thought to get you thinking. Thought leadership and positive statements are good things to make, yet if you follow through, the statement can become so much more powerful. From this position, it is possible to lead, yet you do need to lead them along all the steps.

Horse before cart!

If you focus on the story first, you can look at a story as an overarching theme, as the deliverable, and come up with a whole series of statements from the story. This way around, you will always have a story to follow through with.

For better business storytelling results...

To be clear for the best results, we are talking about non-fiction stories. There are many ideas you can take from fiction to enhance the communication power of non-fiction.

Generally, though, when we look at non-fiction, we will see blocks of text broken into chunks separated by subheads. It is the subhead that could become your posts, statements, and soundbites -and to follow through, get the book - or the movie of the book.

There's an example of a technique you can take from fiction to non-fiction to make a movie of your book. You don't have to make a movie of the whole book. Your movie can be a monologue or a conversation between two or more people and focus on one section or a chapter. It can be published as a short book or as a PDF excerpt.

Your stories are financial assets to add to the balance sheet.

You can see how an idea developed into a story can be a good asset for a business to develop. Assets can be employed repeatedly, plus they have a value and ultimately sit on your balance sheet. Plus, once you have told your story, it is hard for a competitor to tell it. Your stories become part of your intellectual property.

Your story can be personal, personal to you, your business, or personal to your clients and customers. It can also be marketed. The idea of marketing a story is not new. The great news for business is that you can market a story and make it interesting.

The biggest sin in business: to be boring!

Whereas marketing your product or service all the time, especially in a commodity market, can become tiresome very quickly, especially if you operate in an essential area of business, such as tax accounting, for instance, rarely seen as interesting.

Another example of a commodity business area is cyber security, where cyber security is seen by many as an annoyance, technical, dry and, worse, a waste of money. Until your business is taken down by a cyber-attack. However, it can be seen on Amazon. For instance, when it comes to selling cyber security, those books focused on hacking sell a lot more.

Another already referred to is accounting and tax, where the most interesting story in recent years has been the Panama papers.

If you do not focus on market needs, who will?

Of course, you may not wish to be associated with these matters. However, the market is clearly interesting and there is an opportunity. We are in business to serve the market. My recommendation is to give the market what it wants. You can differentiate yourself from the outside cover of your story or within the body text, as you prefer. For instance, you could write a story, as many businesses do: How to avoid being hacked. Or, how to avoid your papers from being leaked like the Panama Papers.

Now those suggestions may not be the ideal headlines or names for a book, yet there have been many statements used which in turn lead to stories your clients are likely to engage with. You might think of them as click bait, for some a derogatory remark. However, all the headlines are, even in the days before you could click, although nowadays it is a real advantage. This can lead to prospects for us.

Hands up all who want clients to come to us

This is the ultimate power of good business storytelling, which leads clients to us. The payoff is that it reduces the cost of sales. Organic and word-of-mouth marketing campaigns can be created, and your story can be passed on, potentially going viral. So much more than a one-off headline or post. Indeed, you can light a fire under a good business story to really get it moving using paid advertising too. Commercially, a good story has everything going for it.

Stories are alive

You can write about your story before it is finished, just as soon as you know what your story will be about. Or you can wait for it to be written and then enter a launch process, launch it, see it through to distribution, then milk it for all it is worth. What you don't want to do is to write the story and put it out there without any conversation, without any build up or anticipation. Chances are your story will fall flat. The process, described in this book is part of the business of storytelling.

Stories die

Eventually, your new story will become old. At which time you can do what Disney does with its' stories. Pull them. Take the story off the market. Later, just as Disney does, you can re-release it, which gives you the opportunity for a relaunch and so the cycle repeats. However, each time your cycle repeats, you can update the story and refer to all the successes and what people said about the story last time.

As you start to understand the power of business storytelling and map your customer journeys, you can change the story, and you can write new ones. You can introduce new characters, new products (ever heard of product placement) or new services and embed them into the heart of your next story. Soon you will have two stories, then three and so on.

Use story to fix a broken business

Your stories become the focus of your marketing campaigns and they focus on your customer journeys where you map out what they get and when. It helps to humanize a business process, which is so often focused on cutting costs and increasing speed that core elements of customer needs are sometimes cut out, or services are discounted to stoke volume, to the detriment of a brand. Yet a good brand story could be exactly what is required to fix what is broken or to make sure the business does not break in the first place.

Use story to stay true to the wider picture

It is important for business owners and managers to always understand their client and customer stories. We want our business managers and owners to think when they want to implement new initiatives, how would that fit into our client story?

Clients and customers don't just pay bills, if we give them what they want, they give us growth, positive experience, and wealth too. All this can add to positive PR. Through this story, we can turn negative planet-destroying businesses to become green recycling businesses, who still manage to grow and give their clients what they want when they want it.

Use story to open new markets

There are some trades, niche businesses, particularly in the military, technical, financial, and insuring sectors, which do not apply to the public. Yet the business goes on and is necessary as they underpin society and so the stories need to be told. It may be the number of readers to be very few, and these are stories often described as something else. A white paper or special report, for instance, or case study. All of these are examples of stories and serve as an example of some of the different types of stories you could tell.

The Zero Moment of Truth

Google coined the ZMOT as the moment when you start researching because you know nothing about the subject. First impressions are important, and this is when the path to purchase could begin if you present an appropriate story for your researcher to follow.

If your business sells expensive or bespoke products and services, or is sold on-line, then it may not be possible to let someone try before they buy, yet you can offer a free guide, white paper, or special report. Something of value for free with little or no friction. Friction is when someone must pay or enter their email address. You can offer a free download that includes links to more information which your readers can sign up for or buy. For instance, consultancy can be sold or given away, depending on how you run your business, both would involve your potential customer needing to register with you.

If you are interested in helping clients find those Zero Moments of Truth, where first impressions occur, lasting impressions are made and the path to purchase is first seen. If you are interested in your market and what researchers find about you, and you are passionate about your marketing and business succeeding, then this book is for you.

You may not be currently found on-line, or you may be top of the search engine rankings. Maybe a salesperson sent out a link, or a post was found that linked to your site. In the next chapter we will focus on what questions your audience asks at each phase of your customer journey, starting with the Zero Moment of Truth.

Chapter 13: Story Openers

Simplicity

Telling stories was one of the first things the human race did. Storytelling is hard-wired into our nature from the earliest times when we lived in caves and likely grunted. What we drew on the walls depicted the stories of the day. We showed them where the animals were, and the knowledge was how, as a species, we survived.

American novelist Flannery O'Connor stated, "I find that most people know what a story is until they sit down to write one."

"Are you sitting comfortably? Then I'll begin"

Those are famous words uttered before every story on Listen with Mother. It was originally a BBC radio program presented from 1950 until sometime in 1996. Millions of children worldwide tuned in.

For many, the triggers of a story are those words. Like "Once upon a time". – has introduced fairy and folk tales since 1380, according to the Oxford English Dictionary.

Whichever set of words triggers our brain; we are all conditioned to listen to stories. When we hear stories, beautiful things happen. We think of happy times when we were growing up. Most importantly, we become physiologically receptive. We expect to tune in and listen.

The thing with a story is that when we realize we are about to hear something interesting, we relax. We have been setting up stories since we were kids. We see the world, human interests and have learned about the world through stories.

The other key attribute of the story is that we see the storyteller as an authority, too, just like our teachers were.

A good story will arrest your attention, cause you to stop what you are doing, and listen in. Stories are more memorable, shareable, and believable.

If you are in marketing and get a solid start to your story, you boost your chances of your business gaining traction. A good tale costs nothing. Powerful stories set trends.

More classic openers

I have a few classic, eminently reusable insider techniques you can use to open your stories.

"Are you sitting comfortably, then I'll begin" and "Once upon a time" are overused, although they can still work. You may prefer to choose from a slightly different pallet, so try these for openers:

Place and date: New York, 2011 You can guess what happened in New York in 2011. However, you can re-use this as a template: Nebraska, 2021.

It is intriguing. Immediately, you wonder what happened. Indeed, you could start with just the place. The Bronks, or: In 1897 … More intrigue, reusable and handy if presenting history or a projection into the future. It all depends on what you want to say. There is flexibility available to you here.

Then, we have the solid sentence. For example: Going to the pub isn't just for the beer; it's a lifestyle. Or: the wealthiest people in the world still look for bargains.

A classic copywriting technique is to open with a question: What does the reader think you can answer? Or, did, you know the average American has less than two weeks' money in the bank?

The controversial opinion opener: Salespeople are born – for those selling sales training. All they need to do is find someone who was born to sell.

The way we sell with stories is to narrow the focus, the more the better.

Conversation starters:

Stories about people are always a lot more interesting to us rather than stories about things. Of course, the story about someone can be about how they were saved by something – the Trojan Horse in action again.

Here are three quick examples:

- I've got a good story.

- You'll never believe what happened to me yesterday

- Did you hear what happened to Janet from Southampton, just last week?

Short Openers – for when space is limited

- Instant Discount
- Tax-Free or VAT-FREE
- Free mobile service
- Sugar free recipes
- One-calorie diet choices
- Lose weight in your sleep
- Look a decade younger
- Fire your boss

Telephone Response:

Thank you for calling, where would you like me to start?

Fortune Cookies

Many firms offer snacks or send responses through the mail. If you do, why not send a personalized fortune cookie? There are many enterprises who will make them for you and many supply them in small as well as large quantities. You could make the message resonate and feature as a conversation starter.

It is always a great idea to offer gifts, and a fortune cookie can inject humor into an otherwise routine situation.

Here are a couple of suggested messages:

- A side: Company name & Logo. B side: Message: Today you will make your fortune.
- 25% off your first order!
- If you sell cars: There is a new car in your future
- Training company: A failure is someone who doesn't try
- Recruitment agency: If you dread Monday mornings, get a new job
- Insurance brokerage: Get the cover you need. Reduce the hassle and loss down the line

116

- Investment opportunity: You will meet new friends on your new venture

How to open a story using social media

In social media or any paid media, space is a premium, so you only have space for a headline.

Headlines introduce stories in a very special way. Where you start from and where you end up. The middle part is the story.

For example: Amazon announces losses for the first time since 2005

The story explains why losses, for the first time in a long time, have been made and what is likely to happen as a result. The headline provides intrigue and possesses the question, leaving you wanting to find an answer.

Here's another:

How a property developer overpaid in the pandemic frenzy – then made a £300,000 loss.

What not to do: be clever

You might be tempted to stop people dead in their tracks with a shockingly simple and clever headline such as "Double or Nothing!" It may sound like a great offer, but your reader has no idea what you are talking about.

These are ego-based headlines. You don't want to use them, they are ineffective.

In real life, you will see people dismiss you, some may even respond with a comment like come back when you have something sensible to say. I have seen that.

Instead, it is better to go with a longer opening headline that your reader can understand. Remember if a reader is confused, they will do nothing, you will lose them all.

Instead, you need to say who you can help. Investors? Lovers? Workers? Who? Chances are you will cut out most readers. On the other hand, you will be seen by the people who count to you.

Tell them what it is about. You want to make life easier for them? Faster? Cheaper?

Finally, you want to specify why. Will it help them with how they feel, how they act? React? What will your reader get in return?

How to go deeper: twist the knife

To go deeper is to extend the outcome. For example: instead of "feel more excited" try "feel more excited, and know your partner is more likely to want to marry you." This is a lot more specific; the stakes are raised dramatically; the reader discovers reading this is extra worth your time.

In effect, you are selling the reader on the future and getting into their heads, so they give you 3 minutes of their time and keep reading or they will be more likely to click on the link as your story is much more compelling.

A word on testing

Most people don't test. They guess. Professional copywriters test. No one truly knows what will work the best. We can all have our favorites, some of us like baked beans on toast, many do not, others might wonder what baked beans on toast are.

The point is we should test and not guess. A test could give us a pay rise.

Copywriters test different headlines and opening statements for all direct mail pieces, and they often test for different things. The main thing they test for is a sale.

If a reader does not respond to your headline or conversation piece, then everything else due to follow will simply not be consumed. No one will know it is there.
In the past, I had a report to offer. I came up with six headlines. I put each on a card and had it laminated. At an event, I asked visitors to choose which free gift I could send to them.

I made sure each headline focused on a different angle of my report. Out of 100 responses, there were two clear winners and one headline that had only three responses. Everybody gave me their email address and everyone got the report, each with a separate covering letter, each covering letter thanked them for taking the survey and told them how their selection was dealt with in the enclosed report.

I also offered a further thank you gift by post (a fortune cookie) if they also provided their postal address.

Although we started by conducting a survey, the report sold them on our service (as well as answering the core question) and the fortune cookie added an additional dimension and touch point.

Most sales were achieved by those who took the survey, read the report, and requested an additional free gift. We also supply them with a slightly deeper level of information and a summary of the original report. The consistency and quality of our headlines and communication did the trick.

We transferred this campaign on-line and achieved similar results, although the responses were far and wide, despite our targeting.

Needless to say, our sales improved, as did the effectiveness of our headlines, and we soon found we had six separate winners and, as time progressed, we produced more tailored reports too.

Chapter 14: Technical Writing Tips

As an eventual author of 14 books, I know if you want to write, all you need to do is write. Yet at first it seems like a mammoth task, impossible, plus who would read what I write anyway?

So yes, as an engineer, the last thing I wanted to do was write. Initially, in every way I thought writing was odd, futile and pointless, yet I kept getting the urge. So, more to prove there was no point and that it required skills I did not have, I sat down at the kitchen table one early Sunday morning with a pen and a few sheets of paper.

I decided to write out a few bullet points. I numbered them, and the points were represented next to the numbers as the lines I had drawn. Unbeknown to me, I created a simple 5-point template. As I stared at it, I figured I should try to fill out the blanks. Starting at first, I figured what the hell and wrote down the first bullet point. I imagined I wanted to teach my newly born son about my business, and it would not be possible if I knew nothing, so I started writing.

My writing was odd, it was all over the place, it did not flow. There were no sentences, some of the points were important, others a lot less so and so I filled out the page.

I made a cup of tea and returned to the table, taking a new blank sheet. I rewrote the first in a better order with some of the minor points underneath the major points. I found that I started to add more points. I hit the dizzy heights of ten major points in about an hour, each with sub points.

Wow, I started to think this thing was starting to take shape. I figured two more major points and I would have a dozen and I figured if I had a dozen, I could call them the down and dirty dozen.

Then I remembered there was a 70s war film with Donald Sutherland called the Dirty Dozen, hey I could write a business book and call it the Dirty Dozen? Could I? Turned out I could, you cannot copyright a book title and as my version of the dirty dozen would be nothing like the film, I would not have to worry about passing off. I never thought much more about it.

I continued to fill in the blanks until I had to use a second sheet as my bullet points and notes were running over. In one case, my notes were more than a sentence, more like a paragraph and as I marveled at what I was looking at, I started to realize that one paragraph could easily become a few more and I could write the same amount or more under each major heading, using the lesser bullet points as a guide. I was literally making this up, as I went along.

Gradually my family appeared and started to gather around the table, they wanted to eat! Who knew it was lunchtime already? It was three hours after I started and now, I had sheets of paper, and tons of notes. It was pretty much in order and made much more sense.

Over the next week or so, I snatched a few minutes here and there and typed those notes into my notebook and discovered, without a lot of effort, I had created my first short book. As I recall, about 7,000 words. I found an artist who made a great cover. I uploaded the whole thing to a self-publishing account on Amazon. I never sold any copies, but I paid for about 30 copies and the book became my new business card and the people I gave it to loved it and asked me to sign it for them too. I don't know if anyone read it. I have discovered how easy writing can be.

Ever since then, although I have employed the odd ghostwriter, I prefer to do my own writing. For me, I find it best to block off time, like the morning or afternoon.

I like writing because I like to discover what I am going to write about. I generally don't know. All I have is an idea, a starting point and then I write either directly or in bullet points. For me, it works, that is my approach.

Great book: On Writing

There are many great books on writing, writing style and so on and some are great, some, for me, difficult. I like and recommend "On Writing" by Stephen King, even though he writes fiction and I do not, there are many rules that are important for both kinds of work. In some ways, I appreciate that fiction is potentially harder than non-fiction, as a fiction reader must believe it is all true, when obviously, fiction is fiction.

I make mistakes, especially when I write

I don't spell everything correctly. I have certain constant grammar issues. Luckily, Word helps and I have a grammar checker. I like to just write, get the ideas out and then fix up (edit) the copy afterwards.

Some common fixes

There are many words, which can be replaced with one word. I just wrote there are many words. This can be edited into many words. "have to" can be replaced by one word: must. I always misspell "their". 90% of the time when I write the word "that" it can be deleted. I learned that from Gary Halbert – a famous copywriter.

Less is more

I used to write in 3–4-hour blocks and I would write thousands of words and then send them over to a friendly journalist who would send them back edited, trimmed down to about half the number. It was depressing. However, I would compare my version to the edited version side by side and see how essential the editing was and how well it was done. Thank you, Caroline.

I still set aside 3-4 hours, but now I write shorter paragraphs and I aim for an entire story to be contained within 250-words. I try to reveal much and avoid repetition. I come from a training background where repetition was key, not so when it comes to writing. A reader can read the same piece again. Where a trainer employs repetition to embed and nail key points down.

Sometimes, I start with a set of key points. For instance, the result of a 250-word block might have a headline, some credibility, followed by 7 key points and a takeaway. That would be a good model. More often it will be 3 points, but occasionally 7. I might then try to write out further 250-word blocks each based on one of the points. 3 to 7 depending. All with an eye to minimize repetition.

With less repetition, potentially your reader will stay interested longer, the more they read, the more value they get and the more you are rewarded as a writer. This is how less is more.

In practice, you would focus on one major keyword, phrase, or bullet point. You would start writing and, if you find yourself veering off. Great, cut it out, save it and use it as the basis for another 250-word block / short article. Get back to where you were and carry on making or supporting your original core point. The more you write, the more you will write.

All in all, what happens is you end up discovering you have considered a key topic from a range of angles and, as a result, you get to write quickly, and you build up a personal body of work on the subject you can re-purpose. In this way, you can afford to focus on a narrow area of the market and keep coming up with good stuff. The alternative is to bluff and bluster until you are found out, not a long-term strategy!

Chapter 15: The simple way to write a story and avoid writers' block and the blank page.

There is much in this book already designed to provide inspiration to write your story.

How to write better stories

I find the idea of writing a story every day leads to better stories. The more you write, the better your stories become.

I can imagine some will shriek no way! I can't possibly write a story a day. That is the point, you will be surprised. The more you write, the more you will write. What happens is you don't run out of things to write about, the more you write, the more things you discover you can write about.

Your first few stories are likely to be a lot of trouble, I will be honest with you, possibly taking an hour or two. It is easy to be put off by this, especially if you say to yourself, you are rubbish, and the evidence proves it. I experienced the same thing.

You will soon discover the patterns

After writing out a few stories, I found a pattern. I started to realize that I pretty much knew what I wanted to write about and who I was writing for. These were my existing and potential customers and as I could see them, I knew where they were, what they were doing and the kind of problems they had.

In effect, I rationalized that as I had the beginning and the end, all I had to worry about was the middle and knowing from where I started, and knowing where I would end, gave me great comfort.

Initially, I just wrote out what I knew.

I did not so much bother with a story, I just wrote out what I knew and afterwards I was surprised at how much that was. I was not surprised that what I had written was a meandering ramble. Something embarrassingly unpublishable.

Yet it was mine, I had written something. I realized that although my writing structure was poor, I did at least have something I could write about. My 'overview', a personal body of work.

I might as well have spoken it out loud. It was written as if I had. That made me realize there is another way to write. I could just record my thoughts into the memo app on my iPhone and that would convert speech to text!

I paid attention only to content, not diction, structure or even grammar, maybe a bit. I was all for just getting my thoughts out and trying to build a picture of what was going on. I could not see how to make a story out of it all, so I did not try. It was a very straightforward approach, and parts of it were initially just bullet points.

The usefulness of the humble bullet point

I employed bullet points as I wanted to write as fast as I was thinking, and I did not want to lose my train of thought. I figured that I could go through and fill in the blanks later. This is exactly what I did. When I felt I had all the angles covered, I went back over my bullet points and added more detail. In many cases, there are more bullet points too.

This is an approach I have taken before and how I wrote my first ever book, which was really an expanded list. It embarrasses me now, although at the time it served its purpose and it won me some business too. The first book was simply a large business card. People marveled over it and were glad to ask me to sign a copy, as the author. I doubt anyone read it, I did not knowingly sell a single copy, which was not what that book was for.

Anyway, with a somewhat muddled picture written out, I had something to work on and I edited and edited and went around and around. At first, I was just trying to make sure things were in a timeline and, where appropriate, added other signs of order, like logical order too. I felt it might be important to see if I could find a way to make my work flow.

Patterns started to appear

I got to where I needed to be and started to realize my big 'story' was an amalgam of many smaller stories.

Also, I started to realize there were certain traits or ideas I had put into practice and repeated. These were unintended, subconscious actions. These could be described as patterns. For instance, in each new business venture, the first thing I did was to go looking for clients and when I found some, I would discover that some would love what I had to sell, others would want me to customize to suit them.

Short stories made sense.

I started to pick one out per day.

I had other things to do and as the 'body' of work was done, all I had to do was look through it and pull one story out and write that out and consider myself finished for the day.

Writing just one story per day gave me time to get on with the rest of my life.

Producing a story each day was the most satisfactory

I started to realize it was possible to tell each of the stories in different ways, for instance, from my perspective, another from the perspective of training how to complete a job and from the perspective of a customer and how I would meet customer expectations. I was writing commercial stories. This is what I was hoping for, and at last it happened.

I also started to limit my time and I quickly found I could write a short 300-word business essay in about fifteen minutes, only if I already had an idea of its' topicality. The more I looked at my initial 'overview', my personal body of work, the more I found short stories, and I also found structure.

Here is a 3-part page prepping structure anyone can use

1 Headline, or title

2 Content bullets. Point #1, #2, #3 etc.

3 Takeaway.

It is a very simple structure where the headline or title is there to both tell the reader what could be coming, ideally a tease to arouse curiosity. We want the reader of the headline to want to know more and, as a result, to want to continue to read.

In the instance above, my headline is: 'Here is a 3-part page prepping structure anyone can use' Followed by 2: Content bullets and in my case 3, as suggested, although it can be 1, it can be many bullet points.

The third part is the takeaway for the reader. The takeaway is what action we would like the reader to take. The writer might propose that some actions should be taken because of the information shared.

Turn your body of work into a larger, more readable story.

Through these eyes, I started to look at my body of work and that is what you now see as part one of this book, my rags to riches story. You will see I used the prepping technique over and over and converted the body of work into 37 short stories, it is included within this book as genuine content to provide insights into just how far you can go into the ins and outs of a founder story and how each may eventually serve a purpose.

The separate reader paths

This part of the book also shows that you can take short stories and, provided they are in context, how they can be joined together to make a larger story. What you may also notice is that this approach causes many subheads to be created, which creates a separate reader's path.

I recently heard the separate readers' path referred to as being especially necessary for on-line readers who read in a hurry, and I am sure that is true too.

Chapter 16: 6 stories you must tell after a sale

If you don't tell a good story, your value may be lost forever, and your recipient will wonder who you are and why you keep bothering them.

It is vital that after an important delivery, whether in the real world or virtual, you follow up with a series of stories. Whether you deliver pdf, word, or excel documents or provide access to membership sites, you want the recipient to be certain, so they recognize the value you have delivered.

Too often, an offer is made, goodies sent and then the emails are not opened, or the goods shelved, or attachment files stored, never to be opened. It may seem unlikely, but most of us forget to use what we have been sent even if we did order and pay for it. This may be due to a late hour, or it is just as likely your recipient gets sidetracked, sometimes by other services or other information you supply.

Letting recipients know after an event can be reassuring to know and provide a valuable link toward doing business again in the future.

1 Delivery

The first story to tell is that delivery has been made.

This can be at the same time as dispatching or the next day. It is up to you, although if it is a digital dispatch, then it is probably better to send the first follow-up story about the dispatch the next day. I.e., did you get it, here's how to find it. Or, if you have dispatched something physical yesterday and you are on the next day's delivery schedule, you can refer to yesterday's dispatch and to today's expected delivery.

Naturally, you should this opportunity to congratulate the recipient on their excellent choice and how you are available to support them.

2 Welcome

This story is about the purpose and application of what has been sent, when and when and could include a copy of the electronic thing being delivered (a link) and a link to the invoice.

Essentially, you make sure the recipient has everything. This will help them if they don't have all they need. This will potentially save customer support time and emails too.

This communication also provides the reasonable opportunity to welcome the recipient to your world, since they made the purchase or request. We should try to build into this story a confetti or celebratory moment. So not just here's your receipt, but you are a winner, aren't you the lucky one to have made such a fantastic choice in choosing us to help you?

We not only want to make the experience a good one, but we also want to do all we can to make their delivery both an unusual and memorable occasion. Perhaps we can send them something extra, either in the delivery box or letter, or by email as part of the follow-up welcome.

This communication is 100% to maintain and develop good will.

3 Reinforce the value

Value reinforcement typically focuses on benefits that arise from the practical application.

A benefit email may link to operating instructions but only references these to focus on the key benefits. This communication is sent to reduce refunds if applicable and to reinforce the value of what you have sent and the value of knowing you. This will help you to be remembered and for other services or products you offer to potentially be evaluated with a more positive disposition toward you. You want your recipients to look forward to your communications.

This communication is 100% to maintain and develop good will.

4 Customer objections

There are many reasons why some people will not buy a product. The reasons are usually connected with time and money.

This communication is to let your customer or potential customer know how you can help them save time and money, perhaps relating to what you have already dispatched, potentially related to other products or services you offer. It supports and follows your good will efforts, and it gently, subtly points towards other ways you can help your recipients, that they may have to buy, or that are included with what they have from you already.

Keep the communication light with a focus on what your service or product achieves. You could start with a reference to its ease of use, or the great answers your service provides to help typical clients achieve something. You can take the opportunity to ask for feedback and that you are constantly in search of new and current case studies and how you would be honored if they became one.

Again, this communication is 100% to maintain and develop good will.

5 FAQ

You will know what the most asked Frequently Asked Questions are for your business.

FAQs most commonly reflect on time and money and can easily relate to technical, practical, or installation-related issues. Again, this can subtly point towards other products or services you supply, while in the first instance, focusing on giving answers to the most common questions.

Again, this communication is 100% to maintain and develop good will.

6 Foreshadow an offer

We are in business, so is never a bad time to sell stuff. We are only delivering on customer needs, and it is through repeat sales to the same customers we develop the best clients.

By now, you may have thought of a follow-up offer, even if you did not have one before. If you prefer, it could be a free offer, which then becomes a paid offer. For instance, telephone support, first hour free.

This means a free telephone support service is available to all while more support is available for a fee. If it gets out of hand or the same customer calls every week and asks the same questions, as some, sometimes do, you can invite them to enter an ongoing service contract. On the other hand, if a customer keeps buying from you, you may want to treat the support calls as sales support and not charge a fee at all, and you can let your customers know the more they buy, the more you will waive the ongoing support fee, as that is how you support valued customers.

In most cases, most customers will not take telephone support. It all depends on a lot of variables, but if you have a good product in a stable market, chances are your clients will rarely call. For most though, it is still nice to know it is available, it is a reason to buy from you as opposed to anyone else and it could make all the difference.

Small hinges swing big doors!

Bonus content: Keep nurturing them

Ask for feedback, share case studies, share how you can help during each season of the year.

Identify new angles. Different customers probably have different use cases.

Let your other clients know what they are doing if this is an acceptable practice in your industry.

You can let your recipients stay in contact through other means or other channels, perhaps via YouTube, or if you have a podcast. One of the better ways to stay in touch with commercial clientele is through the use of printed newsletters and postcards as they tend to be collected.

Part 3: The Founder Story

Chapter 17: Founder story introduction

The founder story is expected and essential. A founder story will voice the core reasons for why your business exists, how it came about and why it should share meaning with the wider world.

First and foremost, we must tell our founders' story in the context of delivering value to our potential customers. The idea of a founders' story is not to write a biography. Some background information could be useful if we can use it to show depth and intention, and more precisely throw light on the kind of problems potential customers face. We want to do demonstrate as much as possible the founder has found a unique and special way to solve customer problems.

These are not likely to be strained stories, or necessarily action/adventure stories, although they could be, it depends on the reality of them and on the background of the founder and who they serve. For instance, if you serve extreme rock climbers, then a story about the extreme experience of the founder would not be out of place.

For me, the adventure was the business, the ongoing risk, and the calculated nature of it all. Yet at the same time, it was all good humored, there was certainly stress at times, but very little was negative about my adventures. The negatives were largely all mine, based on the decisions I made, I suffered my own responsibility. They were of my own doing. Some of my adventures were traps I fell into by accident. Once bitten, twice shy!

There was a time when I either put food on the table or I paid the rent. I paid the rent. I made the decision to take on a lease and it was my decision to stick to it. I could have reneged on the deal and done a runner. However, I did not want to be a loser and I did plan to honor the commitment I had made. That is what I refer to when I say I took risks and responsibility.

What I don't say too often about that food and rent story, is that instead of food, I chose beer. I went to the pub. I chose to cheer myself up rather than have TV dinners and get lost in the downward negative spiral of the daily news. It went on for a while, and I missed out on quite a lot of the news. I also gave up smoking, so it was not all bad!

First however, I want to share the approach you see many politicians take when they get to speak to crowds large and small and how they get people on board who don't know them. There are techniques you may like to borrow, should you find yourself needing to give a presentation to a group of people you don't know for the first time.

The following chapters relate directly to exactly what happened to me and how events unfolded. In the first I was on the up and up, the second I faltered a little and in the third I got back on the horse I had fallen from and rode again once more.

Little miracles did happen, and they were largely of my own making. What I hope you take away from this is the fact there are stories in almost everything you do. They make up who you are.

Once you live them, there is no reason why you should not talk about them and rather than live off parables and ideas of the past, written by others, you will find you really do have your own stories to tell and share.

These chapters are written as prompts to help you find the places where stories exist within you and my examples are provided not to share my story particularly, but more to inspire and help to highlight where your hidden gems might be located, where your miracles occurred. By sharing some of my vulnerabilities, you may realize it could be OK to share yours.

Please grab a pen or pencil and some paper and note how these stories could help you recall your personal history, so you can share your stories with a world who just can't wait and is ready to hear them.

Chapter 18: The Founder Presentation

When a founder needs to tell the story and introduce something new, we would do well to reference famous speeches presented by up-and-coming politicians. We are not concerned with their politics, but the choice of topics and flow are worthy of consideration.

Politicians often start with how they are as grounded as their audience, which makes sense, as we want people to imagine we are like them. So, we should start by talking about familiar places, locations or activities that relate to real life and as normal an upbringing as possible.

Incredulously, I once heard a CEO stand up and talk about her private education, her big house, her collection of German cars and, amongst other things, the cost of the diamond-encrusted dog collar she bought for Scutchy, her chihuahua, wore. She was very proud of her achievements and how she expressed her love for her dog and expected applause. They said it was a tough gig, her speech went down like a lead balloon, and she was booed off the stage. I felt sorry for her, but she had got to this point through a gilded path and had clearly not met ordinary people.

Relate to be more than just liked

You must be relevant to your audience and win them over.

You want your audience to dig what you do, not just like you. Sounding nice, dressing well, and looking good is a start, but not enough. Relevancy could be summarized in one word: Backstory. It is a tough one, as, for instance, my backstory spans decades, and no matter how many it spans, when delivering our story, we only have minutes to share our tale.

This may seem like a gargantuan problem to have. How can we possibly condense decades of fun into mere minutes? Fortunately, it forces simplification on us. We must pull out the key points, and they must be relevant to our audience too, as we want to ensure our audience relates.

The answer as to what we pick for our backstory relates to how well we know our audience. In the case of writing out a story to be read, we probably know little to nothing about our readers. Indeed, those readers may well be the other side of the world from us.

146

Start with how you grew up, education or parents

These are not the only topics, joining clubs, getting involved, might be more appropriate, but probably not my first girlfriend story. I have heard a few over the years and they can make you want to hide and have the opposite effect to the one we want.

Most will have had some form of education, although it is not guaranteed 100% will have and, of course, education can be delivered in all manner of ways, so I like to keep it vague.

Many people take a bus to school, many never did. I certainly did not and a few years ago I was delighted to finally get inside my first all-American big yellow school bus. I had only seen them in films before, and it was as tatty and as nasty and firm as I thought it would be. While nearly everyone else present reminisced I just enjoyed the experience.

However, I would not talk about transport, or the school in any detail or even the location or surrounding countryside, in fact, it is an advantage to keep it vague. The more vague, the shorter that part of your presentation, the more likely the audience is likely to imagine us together at their school. Exactly what we want them to do.

We want to put our audience in an imaginary environment where they would most likely be familiar with us. This will help develop rapport as they start to think we are talking to them, there.

Hopefully, you are starting to see how this works. We build out our introduction by including familiar places where familiarity is in the eye of our audience and the likelihood is they will then place us with them there, or at least associate us with those warm, happy, and fuzzy memories. I am not just being romantic here. This is what happens, this is important, this is how we build relationships. This is how we get people onside.

Once I have a familiar location placed in the mind's eye, I can layer in what happened, how the subjects I learned (as you did) influenced the rest of life and led us to do what we do now. This underlines the lifelong depth of journey and underscores the shared issues important to our audience.

New and improved are favorable topics

People like to hear about what's new. If we present our life as a lifelong learning journey, we will not look like we know it all. Make what we do new and improved, I am all for that. Having said that, I have probably just connected with a larger number of my audience. I could also include references to acts of valor, courage, even happy accidents, luck, and serendipity, these all have their place, you must be in it to win it, right?

Stand for fairness

When it comes to considering the issues, we may decide and declare we stand for certain values. Given an issue, we must show we always err to the side of fairness. To be reasonable as part of our values, is a good look. Having and standing by our values shows that we are not the kind of person to turn a blind eye. This is how we show that we are also reliable. Three strong values.

Speak and write all I might, not everyone pays attention to everything.

When your audience connects will vary

Each of the elements so far can be the trigger for your audience to want to support you.

Some will jump on board very early, as they may be quick to decide they like you and want to support you no matter what you stand for, as it is bound to be good.

Others will connect with you en-route, while others will stand off and deliberately decide to wait until the very end before they make any commitment either way. They either want to hear the full story before they will commit or, in many cases, they will want to see how they think the rest of the audience feels.

Purpose

By speaking about values as they relate to issues, we set ourselves up to have meaning and that leads neatly into the next part of this business-building framework: Purpose.

148

Purpose directly maps the impact we could have and calls for support from your audience who find they share things in common with you. They may have faced similar issues and have determined there are certain values they may have never considered before they can see themselves supporting.

What is nice, for your audience, is it may appear you are not asking the audience to do anything other than to support you as the speaker, yet at least. As a result, if you can relate to the person delivering the message, if you can see the issues faced and can see the purpose and potential impact, why would you not support this?

Will your story raise emotions?

Emotions are the ultimate lightening rod through which we can connect.

If this was the first time hearing such a message, your audience may wonder why they had not heard of this before and, in part, may feel outraged. Certainly, it is possible that we may reach an emotional crescendo as we near the end.

We are not yet finished, but we are near the final moments. As we outline the issues, build on the foundation we have relayed, and share some of the values we feel are important, we should have our audience feel the same way.

We will have followed a natural, logical process and got towards the inevitability of purpose and the potential impact. Now, we can speak more clearly about our Vision. When our vision is shared and mapped through to the presentation already explained, we can finally speak to this last component: Strategy.

Strategy is a logical step that should naturally flow. We may have hinted as we got here, now we actively co-opt the key truths already pronounced and show our audience how they can contribute to the successful conclusion of the vision by playing a part in the future strategy of implementation.

Your strategy of implementation should include a series of participatory levels, ranging from lending a voice to lending a hand, to being more active, to making an investment and supporting a program financially, or simply voting in support of the program you have in mind.

Whatever you do, you must ask and have asked and explain what and why you can thank and bring proceedings to an end. There are many ways to end, and you could include them all. You can ask open-ended questions, you can list options, you can leave your audience with powerful thoughts. Ultimately, you want to tease your audience into wanting more. To get more, it is not over for them to take the next step and you feel no qualms in letting them know this is the case.

Finally, you should get applause. Take it. Don't rush off, it might look like you don't care. Instead, stand still, look into the eyes of the audience, and thank them, thank them again and keep on thanking them. Perhaps, after a reasonable time, if you have not already, you can intimate or say you will be available outside and that it is time to make way for the next speaker.

Chapter 19:
Avoiding 'death' by PowerPoint!

There is more than one way to deliver story and sometimes your story may be a pitch, and it is possible you may use slides, in which case you will most likely use a PowerPoint presentation. The issue is how to avoid the 'death by PowerPoint' syndrome, and win the day.

The syndrome is occurs when a team has been reviewing presentations all day and every one has used PowerPoint. So it is not hard for your presentation to be considered boring or difficult to listen to. The pain can be so heart felt by your audience they feel like they want to commit hari cari (whatever that is).

The subtext of this story is how and why you must sit at your client's side whenever possible. Also your presentations must make sense. Interestingly, the solution for each is related to the story you want to tell and so it provides further source ideas for the story itself.

Presentation teams

Usually, when you are presenting to an audience, they sit on one side, you sit on the other. You present to the audience and somehow you need to communicate in such a way for them to buy in. My problem is this 'normal' approach can be extremely confrontational, and dialogue is often one way.

On more than one occasion, I have presented to clients using PowerPoint from the bright lights of a stage where the lights were so bright it was impossible to see the audience. These are disadvantages which must be overcome.

I have found two ways to overcome them. Circumstances vary, but if I am part of a presentation team, then I allow my best presenter to present and other members of the team and I, the most senior the better, sit on the audience side and communicate with each other by running a private chat application through our earpieces and mobile phones. This is not always easy to do, but it can be done.

Essentially, the presenter presents a certain conversation point. We know what they will be in advance and wait for them to come around. Those of us on the team, sitting with the clients among or next to us, will clap and congratulate from our seat so our potential clients can hear our enthusiasm without raising our voices and we will, of course, smile and turn to the clients, hoping to create an infectious smile wave. Often it works. Then we nod and say something like "don't you agree" often, again. So, we now have an agreement. Expect to get caught out, you have to agree and see it through, it usually works to get most onside.

First, knowing there are a few conversation point setups, we will communicate prompts to our presenter, who probably can't see us to carry on, and the presentation will pace with potential customer conversation. Maybe at the next conversation point, or perhaps a few more, having gained even more commitment from the audience that we (the presenter) are on the right track, we might just say this directly and again, seek agreement and then, from within the audience, ask a nice big open question, along the lines, of: I love you are loving this, what is the best bit do you think? What is the part that is going to help your business the most? What is likely to be the biggest impact?

I might ask those questions one at a time or all together. The potential customer will tell us and for clarity we will let the presenter know who is on the group call, I will repeat the biggest things. Like magic, our presenter will now weave these new facts in the presentation. Invariably, we will get the business.

Single person presentation

Another way, where there is a lit stage, but no team, I will leave the stage and try to present from the audience provided I can carry the mic, so I will control the slides with an electronic wand and talk to the crowd at the event from the audience side.

This makes me more accessible, and some people will tend to join in with me with some banter if I am lucky and I will be able to laugh, joke and potentially play with the audience. It can make all the difference to the take up of your offer, when you make one, and you always should.

Most business situations that use PowerPoint lose.

Usually, presentations contain too much information, the audience reads the slides, is distracted by them, and then doesn't hear the words of the speaker.

Yet you can still use PowerPoint!

Use fewer words

Open with the promise

Get the objective and preferably the outcome into the open as soon as possible.

As your audience arrives, as they get comfortable, as introductions start, everyone should not only be clear of the purpose of the meeting but also the desired outcome. You should use an image and the image should be in context and create a warm feeling.

Use warm slides

Too often the slides scream emergency, whereas we want to deliver a calm solution. Photographs showing conflict may be too dramatic, we are not running a horror show. I have tested this and know it is a mistake. Even if the audience is alarmed, they want to be calmly informed you can solve the problem.

Tell a story

Overall, the opening slide enables the presenter to tell a short story about the reason why we are ideal placed to solve the problem.

Most presenters focus on supplying statistics to prove a point, data points, unfortunately are easily forgotten, often misinterpreted, and can come into question while only being memorable if your audience writes down the numbers.

Whereas stories have a better recall, and tend to be believed.

Tests have shown that data is remembered less than 5% of the time, whereas a story is more likely to be remembered over 65% of the time. A big advantage.

Your first slide answered what. Your internal slides should answer the who, why, and how. You can sneak in slide pairs if you really want to spell it out, but the more you add, the harder it will be to convey your message. Less is more. You can hand out show notes of the key conclusions you want your audience to remember. Less really is more.

If you have data, it would be best to have it printed separately, hand it to each delegate and refer to it as part of your story. Just remember data is likely to be questioned and doubted, data is rarely your friend. Also if you have been invited to pitch, do you need to prove anything at all, only that you are the best supplier and you are most able to look after their interests.

Story is memorable, and it gives the opportunity for your personality to enter the room. Your audience will understand more about who you are for them. This will add to your credibility and effective power.

Use story to introduce them to you and focus on the promise.

Use very few slides

Use no more than three slides for your content if at all possible.

Yes, use very few slides.

If you use more than a few slides, you will be delivering what is commonly known as 'death by PowerPoint'. This is especially true if you are meeting a group who are presented to often and who have seen slides all day. The less professional will use tons of slides and pack them with detail. You want to be known as the team with the best slides.

Your slides want to show pleasant, large, warm, glossy, yet appropriate and relevant images that make the point. Ideally with a single headline. A talking point. As presenter, you will tell a short story about the slide.

Fewer slides = more story = more understanding = more trust.

One slide is all you get at the end, anyway

Like the other slides, you should use a good quality contextual image where the text on the slide simply states when. This slide is a placeholder for your story. It will contain just a few words. Less is more. The messaging from all the slides will be simple and comforting.

Each slide captures the attention and relates to the objective in context. As a result, all eyes will be on the presenter and the story being told will be heard.

The temptation is to prove an idea or concept, whereas the objective is to decide. If further proof is required, it needs to follow an objective decision and that can be the subject of a later customer presentation, that is unless they specifically ask for data. If they don't refrain from using data as it is easily forgotten, easily questioned and can cause loss and delay. No. Data.

Chapter 20:
Rags to Riches

How a young apprentice earned millions for 100s of blue-chip clients in London

In 1983, I was in search of a miracle. Having finished my apprenticeship as an electronics design engineer trained in missile guidance technologies, I decided I preferred working with people and entered the freelance world. I undertook a few highly-paid short-term contract assignments that quickly became more and more commercial. Things started to happen.

Within five years, I had moved from military electronics design to IT marketing, and my approach was fresh. I had no prior opinions; I had not studied marketing. I just had an affinity for the work, and I enjoyed talking about it.

Since I understood the technologies involved, I communicated well with clients and picked up many technical marketing projects. Over the next few years, my personal development turned into many distinct and separate stories. Some made no sense at the time. Now the picture is clear.

Doing something different

I pioneered telephone marketing for businesses when people said I should not. I had not read any business or marketing books. I was young. It made sense to do something different.

I acquired a series of agency and design clients, then Ernst & Young and Lloyds Bank.

Personal Invention

As a young apprentice, it wasn't easy to stand out among the many engineers around me. I wanted out from the bottom of a testosterone-infested heap.

A keyboard that arrived in the post was among the random goodies at the R&D lab where I worked. It was unsuitable for our purposes, as plastic melts at high temperatures. Happily, I attached the keyboard to my Sinclair home computer.

I could see this was my ticket out if I could sell thousands of them.

My first sales

I would turn up at a computer store with a couple of boxed computer keyboards under my arm and ask to see the manager. I demonstrated how they worked and suggested I leave them there.

The shop could sell them for $55 and owe me $35. The profit was a generous $20. Impressed, the shop owner or manager invariably agreed. I paid $14 per keyboard – a win/win deal.

Sure enough, we all made money. I would call the manager/owner and get a follow-up order. Then I would ask the retailer to pay in advance for new stock. As I was in my 20s without cash, I needed payment upfront. That was my first business story.

I connected by turning up. I engaged by taking a risk and inspiring the shopkeeper to buy more after selling the products. Once a shopper who overheard our entire conversation and watched the demonstration purchased the item before I'd even left the store.

We all loved it when that happened!

The messy business

I sold thousands of keyboards over a messy three-year period.

Messy, as I made everything up as I went along. While it worked out fine, I appreciate not everyone has this kind of success.

Economic factors were on my side since I had no office, no shop, no storage, and initially, the stock was from free samples. I asked for more to 'test.'. No costs and no fear of loss. Just a simple idea. It was fun. I scored a hit.

We sold keyboards in the UK, Europe, and. Australia at trade fairs and other events. I was regularly receiving and processing batches of 100s of keyboards.

The business lasted three years, and I needed to take stock. I bought a Porsche 944 sports car and managed not to kill myself or get arrested.

Telemarketing

I decided to set up a telemarketing agency business, so I would not need cash for stock.

It was clear other business concerns did not know how to get new business. To me, it was just a matter of phoning, running a demo, and putting a deal together with a reseller. Many needed that service.

Ironically, I won the Ernst & Young Entrepreneur of the Year awards program as a 'long-term' contract. It was a poisoned chalice, but I didn't know better.

I launched the program by phoning and asking companies if they would like to win the award. The program went global and survives to this day.

I also won a contract with Lloyds Bank and several design agencies – just as I had committed to a tight five-year lease. Before these wins, I had to either pay the lease or buy food. I opted for the former. We kicked it off and made it work. It was tough, but we came through. We did not starve for long.

Investing in me

A few years passed, the end of the lease renewal loomed into view, and I had no plans to renew.

I started to look for other business opportunities and reluctantly left an unfurnished office fully furnished with an air conditioning and a fully functioning telephone system.

Buying, processing, and selling stock was exceptionally risky as it was so cash-intensive, albeit profitable. I always had to buy more stock than I had orders for and amortized R&D costs for tooling and customization over the first few thousand keyboards. The profits of that business were only realized at the very end, a long slog.

Then I signed up for a five-year lease, which pushed from one long-term commitment to another. I figured I needed ample space to run a telemarketing business. Plus, when I started, I was comforted with hard cash. It took the first two years to sort that out. And things were tight, very tight.

In early 1996, while running a telemarketing business, the internet appeared. It just so happened, I had to send myself off from London to LA to an event called X factor, all about business optimization, where I met Michael Basch, the founder of Fed Ex, who told a moving story.

His story moved me and the audience to tears. I realized how many (true) stories I had experienced and how important they had been to my life's success. I contacted Mike via LinkedIn the other day.

The Internet

On the way home from the US, I decided I no longer wanted to be in business optimization. I wanted to be in the world of web optimization, which I figured had more fantastic elements.

Back then, the web was slow and just taking off. The new big thing! I wished that I could help improve it and get involved in some way. I changed the name of my business to Weboptimiser.

Weboptimiser ran for nearly 20 years. We were in a variable-sized 100% serviced office with a one-month get-out clause. No stock. No 5-year commitment. With furniture, with a telephone system and air-con too! Perfect. Available in all major cities now.

There was one search engine, Altavista, followed by hundreds more. Now there's Google.

The first client

I attended a meeting in Newbury with the sales director of Bayer Pharmaceutical. He had heard what I was planning and wanted web optimization. I listened and took note of his specific requirements. I paid attention, said I could do it and would return with a proposal.

I left the meeting calm and collected on the outside. Utter panic was trying to break out from the inside. What? How? Yet I was determined. With my knowledge of electronics and knowing how to hand-code an early microprocessor, I could work out how to give Bayer what it wanted.

I was right to think there was a future in this.

Bayer Pharmaceutical was my first ever search engine marketing client.

For the next few years, we were pioneers. There was no one else, no one to copy or emulate. We set the standards, and we had the name before anyone else. Our name has become ubiquitous within the industry.

We were telling stories all the time. Content is always king. We would take a keyword and stuff it everywhere repeatedly. Search engines seemed to like it.

I had migrated from the keyboard to keyword!

Chapter 21: Beyond the keywords to story

To migrate from the keyboard to the keyword was quite a leap.

Next, I quickly found myself working out how to apply story ideas for developing our own new business and coping with failure and rejection. You can't back winners all the time.

The story story

Stories became our weapon of choice!

We started writing news stories and publishing press releases that made sense. We hoped the content would be keyword dense and exciting to web visitors. We would help clients find stories or construct them to appear suitable. Some would be competition-led, others would be challenging; the point is to include the keywords we wanted but be fun and engaging.

As we worked with more prominent branded clients, it was essential to employ contextually appropriate stories. Our clients did not want their websites to look stuffed with keywords. It looks unsightly, and it is not a good website visitor experience. Imagine if every third phrase here was a business growth story. Ha!

At the time, this knowledge was significant, and the story, as it turned out, was our edge. We attracted a full A-Z range of branded clients, from Adobe to London Zoo.

We found that more and more clients wanted stories and, like us initially, they knew very little about the importance of stories or how to use them on-line.

Naturally, the story still applies today, particularly with the advent of social media!

The Panster

All my life, I have been a panster – a person led by the seat of his pants. It also refers to a class of writers. Many like me act first and ask for forgiveness later. Most of the time, taking action worked out well.

It works for me to have a vision, although I must have the end in mind to proceed. Faced with an idea without an ending, I write it out; otherwise, the concept will likely fail in the real world.

I might have a half-baked story, I think, is a good idea, yet it remains half-baked until the end of the story is understood. This system creates a process that avoids risk, unnecessary expense, and wasting time.

A panster is not afraid to try different things. Equally, you must also be prepared to admit defeat from time to time and close things down as fast as they started. It is all about trying and with the best will in the world; sometimes, the end you have in mind is not feasible.

Knowing that something will not work can be as valuable as discovering something that does. One route is very profitable, while the other reduces costs. You make money in business by reducing costs and increasing sales. It's called failing forward.

The most important story

I know now, for instance, before any action, I must work out the story of what I will do before taking action.

I would jump in beforehand, and the wrong kind of story might unfold. I have seen too many people lose their shirts through incredible financial loss because they did not think their story through. We are easily carried away by excitement and anticipation of potential.

Take the time to think.

The 'build it, and they will come' strategy

I still see people new in a business stroll up, chest proverbially puffed, taking enormous risks. Stories provide a process and mechanism to think. It is essential to determine a strategy and see it through.

The 'build it, and they will come' strategy invariably fails.Equally, many improve their skillsets without benefit. They suffer from frustration without a future story because they don't deliver despite their skills, knowledge, and willingness.

Few ever get to utilize that knowledge. Few customers, or employers, will appreciate it. It can become challenging to earn a living even if you have the skills and can't share a good story.

A good business story involves a supplier finding customers who pays. We hope to develop a good story, yet sales do not necessarily occur.

I am all for being in service and helping potential clients out. However, at some point, you need to make a sale. You can't just give stuff away. Sales fail to materialize too often, and it is not sustainable.

Be sure of where sales will occur before you invest.

The story template

Be inspired by a dream, but think your story through before you leap into investing time, energy, and treasure.

We know the beginning, where you are. We can see the middle – what you are about to start. Now, think about the end. Is the end where you want it to be? Does the middle part lead you to the end? It does? All good. It doesn't? What can you change?

You must take what you do to the market, and the market must grasp the opportunity instantly and buy into your offer. For employed directors, sales, and marketing managers, the worst that can happen is you can lose your job. Thus the default position for many is to do nothing or minimize risk at best.

I would recommend the same for business owners too. Most people do little to nothing if they cannot see a strategy. Please don't be ashamed; it is very wise.

Your story needs to be developed and thought through to the end before anything else.I am looking for the cheapest way to test. Invariably, during the test process of talking to potential customers, you discover what they want, and only then will you have a sale.

Your final test question must be: would you pay for this?

Understand your story outcome to develop a strategy

Determine your objectives first.

If you can see a good story outcome, you will have determined what you want; you can divine a strategy to achieve your objective.

You should include the part that limits your exposure to risk too. Test it. Build a minimum viable product and go ask a client to buy it. Part of your test is finding and being very clear about who your customer will be. Work this out in advance and include it as part of your objective so you can plan a strategy accordingly. It can be tough to do for the first time, sometimes, it is evident, yet it is always vital.

I had an idea years ago. I listened to a podcast recently, and the discussion reminded me of my past thoughts. This time I figured I would build it, as now I could see the end of the story, and the strategy just came to me.

I wrote some simple code to test one of the main features and set it up on a subdomain, and it worked. No cost. I then bought a domain https://soichio.com, and it sits there now while I develop two more features. The total amount invested is about $15. Hosting costs nothing on Amazon AWS.

I can use this development in three different ways, and it is good enough to start. I am not ashamed or upset that the other parts are incomplete. Neither have I put everything else on hold to go for hell to leather to complete it all.

I look forward to spending a few more hours developing it.

Success at little cost, now that's a story everyone loves!

So why this story, why now?

First, I am keen you should know I have not simply been on a writing course and became excited enough to write a story for story's sake.

My founder's story, although largely accidental, worked out. I was able to think, strategize, and convert a range of different ideas into action. It was not about getting lucky; it was about execution, starting and stopping, depending on how things worked out. The more I fail, the closer I get to success. It took a lot of effort, and I had to gain familiarity with unfamiliar territory. Who doesn't?

I keep referring to the story; this is a book about storytelling for enterprise; this is my founding story and out of it, as you can see, are many short stories that make up the whole.

If I had not sweated the small stuff, the big stuff would never have happened.

You can do the same; you really can. Just start something.

The failure & survival story

Life has not been plain sailing. I accumulated some wisdom and located treasure.

I am keen to share to help others, partly as a thank you to all those that helped me.

I have learned much the hard way. I am happily twice divorced. Yet here we are. You, too, can thrive and survive!

There is something in this for me, too

By writing and reviewing, I understand the importance of these personal events even more.

For instance, I coach, run mastermind groups, produce digital products, write newsletters, and have a small but exciting following. It is all relatively modest. However, I am asked for my opinion and advice daily. So, I had better be clear in my head!

However, importantly, to paraphrase an earlier quote, I don't know what will happen until I write it out and put it out there. Being positively intentioned, I expect good things; who knows. What could go wrong? The question is, what will I remember doing? What ideas will it spark for my readers, customers, and clients?

There are also opportunities, as I found in my last book, 'How to start a business without any money, where I wrote out 42 growth hacks. I realized many more growth hacks in other areas.

If readers liked those growth hacks, I figured they might like this focus on stories.

A list is not a good enough story

From the last book, some asked for just the list of hacks.

I figure some might ask for a list of the different story types in the future.

I supplied a list of hacks, and the same people asked for explanations. I referred them to the book. I don't give out the list anymore; get the book.

However, I share the list via a series of TikTok videos. Many folks have been buying the book as a result.

I may do the same with the stories here, too – individual TikToks with an explanation.

The TikTok story

I record a daily 15s TikTok video (which I enjoyed, mainly as it takes little more than 15s to do).

The 15s TikTok video would be quickly seen by about 500; then, a batch would be seen by 250. Just when I thought it would dwindle further, it peaked at 650 for a first-day exposure. The number of TikTok videos I produce grows daily, 15s at a time! I see more and more new likes every day too, as the numbers steadily rise.

The more I do, the more comments I get, the more sales I make, yet it only takes me 15s a day. It's the best!

Again, people asked for more information.

Within the 15s video, I started adding an extra line by explanation. Again I received messages asking for more. Thank you. Again, I refer them to the book.

A simple list of growth hacks is not enough; explanations become more memorable if described in some form of context: story!

In other words, even on TikTok, we see the inescapable application of the story associated with the strategy.

I hope you get loads from the stories in this book.

I hope you understand, absorb, and apply the growth strategies I share, some or all of them. You probably realize they have all come from applied experience. You can use this playbook for reference.

They are not just hacks, but standards I apply, biblical!

Sometimes it is essential to provide a signpost in the middle of things to let readers know where we are and why we have got here.

These are real stories; they are not the most perfect or ideal stories. They may lack color, although they all add up to authenticity. The idea of recalling these stories is primarily to highlight the importance of simple everyday events that happen and how you can pull stories out of them.

Stories don't need to be complex or dense; they must be shareable and easy to follow.

Chapter 22: Bigger Pictures

This part is a collection of bigger picture stories that share opportunities, dangers, and how to avoid them.

The gold in the old

Many new to marketing come in with a particular leaning. Mine was relationships through story development driven by keywords.

For the past few decades, digital has framed marketing. Yet big enterprises spend their marketing dollars mostly on 50% TV and 50% Digital.

Digital marketing is more variable and measurable than TV.

However, the issue is not the media but rather how what you are promoting will interest the customer. If you cannot connect, you will not inspire people to buy. You will spend money and not sell anything.

To connect, you need to be able to tell good stories. Copywriters are worth studying to provide insights.

Forget about the media story!

Let's put it another way. If someone took away the media, where would you be?

If you had tapped into human nature, you'd most likely have a portable campaign that would work on any media and reach your audience's hearts no matter where they are.

Print and digital both use direct marketing. It is why you still get offers in the post. Of course, printed media is more expensive and takes longer, but it puts paper into the hands of your audience, stays around longer, and works in isolation. Results are, therefore, arguably better with print.

Most big retailers publish catalogs because consumers take them and they drive traffic. Digital printing and user IDs are more customizable to suit individual customers.

Let's burn a hole in your pocket story

Universally members and existing customers are rewarded with money off vouchers.

A money-off voucher is like cash to a rabid buyer. It may help customers consume more, inflate your currency and bring new customers into the fold.

A voucher burns a hole in the pocket, encouraging instant spending. The retailer gives you a few cents off a product, an extra hour, or bonus treatment to draw customers into the store, hoping you will buy other things while you are there.

These promotions do not cost anything; they reduce line profits. Perhaps other lines are sold, so they still make on the rest if they lose 10% from one item.

You can make offers by mail and on-line, but on-line many other proposals can be found cheaper.

Whichever way you deliver your voucher, you'll find most sales occur as the offer closes. So on-line, if someone ignores your bid, you have their email address; you can at least remind them.

The commonly held view

Someone else's worldview can be unpacked, revealed, and used to connect with people and bridge the tale you want to tell that relates to your enterprise.

A familiar worldview is that advertising is expensive with no guarantees. Many in business feel advertising wastes money they can ill afford. Taking that line will connect with many. If you sell advertising, this story is the elephant in the room.

You will likely reach an agreement when you raise this point early in your sales pitch. Then you can present a case to show why your angle is different. You cover the other benefits of your offer, and the fear of loss will recede as the value piles up. Benefits could include editorial exposure, sponsorship of the website or an upcoming event, and overall exposure to the market.

Commonly held views usually are reasons not to buy. The best we can do is deal with them first, minimize or neutralize their effect and overwhelm with additional value.

The feelings story

Feelings and emotions have a fantastic impact on sales presentations.

Since direct marketing has been around for tens of decades, there are recognized masters of the art. Notably: James Web and his A Technique for Producing Ideas. There are also the Robert Collier letters, the thoughts of David Ogilvy, and now the late Joseph Sugarman and his classic, Triggers. These are books you can search for on Amazon. The masters tell us it is all about feelings and how we must tap into human nature.

Indeed, we should tap into human nature through each step if we want to connect, engage, and inspire. When you think in this way, the media becomes irrelevant. You don't just advertise; you tell a story; stories capture the attention. Pitch time is storytime.

I sit client-side as often as I can rather than stand upfront and present. My focus is always on the emotional content or meaning to the audience.

You can present yourself as an engaged witness for the most powerful presentations.

The Danger, Will Robinson story

Be careful what you ask for.

In the Lost In Space TV series Will Robinson is the main character and his robot was always predicting danger. Predictions of danger are a powerful motivator and can work to dangerous effect. Yet danger can open significant opportunities and do a lot of good too.

I have met a few competitors who had a story to tell with neither substance nor significance. There are two dangers to this. First, you can look stupid, and secondly, saying one thing and delivering another is known as bait and switch. It's not a good look.

If you draft a great story and the product or service that follows is poor, you come across as a fraudster. You're in danger of earning a bad reputation.

Spend more time on delivering a great story before you launch anything.

The Nazi regime is another example of how a powerful story can cause an entire nation to exterminate a section of the population. Goebbels said the more extensive the lie, the bigger the story. The chances are you will lose everything and cause destruction in your wake. That has happened just about every time. There is no point.

Negative storytelling has moved entire countries to their destruction. Poor storytelling often appears in our daily news and politically orientated media outlets as propaganda.

These adverse outcomes show how powerful storytelling can be. I have had people use stories to coerce me to do things. When influential people flex muscles in these circumstances, the best you can do is to walk away. Compromising pulls you right back in, and an inch soon becomes a mile.

Maintaining your integrity and honesty is better than losing them.

The purpose story

When engaging through empathy, you must share the negatives and the positives.

Knowing that customers always look to overcome negatives, I always start with the negatives. If something is cheaper elsewhere, it might take longer or not result in a good fit.

You probably recognize the story because the outcome is so common.

The buy-in from story

Many of us need to get buy-in from more than one person, whatever your intent.

For instance, a client may need to feel specific positive outcomes to buy into the ongoing story.

Some concerns go wrong such as when an agenda changes or an essential part breaks. It would help if you got people onside quickly. Unless you have provided updates on progress and prepared your audience, they could react angrily and create additional difficulty.

It is vital to harness traditional storytelling to limit the potential damage in these circumstances. One method to limit the damage is to tell the ongoing story through the good times and to let your readers know of certain dangers that could arise.

The arrest of story

A good story can stop you in your tracks.

The structures of stories from the East and West are fundamentally different. The western story tends to create and celebrate a hero. Eastern stories focus on the community's actions, outcomes, and joint celebration. In the east, it is important culturally for people to work together. A culture of independence and personal ability is nurtured more in the west — significant differences.

Think about your audience if you want to use a story that arrests attention. I learned the importance of this as I had a base in central London where you can find customers from the west and east in the same city.

So, remember to tune your story depending on whether you communicate with people from western or eastern hemispheres.

Uses and applications of story

Uses and applications include feeling good about yourself, your future, the future of others, and indeed the past.

One of the exciting things about stories, often overlooked when examining people in the past, is that they can describe good and bad things, trauma, and delight.

Good does not have to triumph over evil; there are terrible true stories where bad gets worse. These stories can serve as a warning to others.

For instance: don't step over the edge; you'll die. Someone did.

Educational story

Stories can also be educational, and this is the central area of the story you will find in this book, tuned to enterprise application areas.

Educational and enterprise stories include references to good and bad outcomes. Manipulative stories have short shelf lives.

If you had the intelligence and ability to write any story, why not produce one to focus on the positive? Why not help others?

Your chances of succeeding with a good story are greatly enhanced, and its longevity may magnify opportunity.

A good story

A good story can stop people in their tracks, grab their attention from whatever they are doing and let them in on a secret or little-known fact.

With a story, you can share a joke and draw people into your world.

People thank you when you share a good story.

The business story

The business story has big applications in sales and marketing, even though many commercial organizations see factual stories as fiction and miss out. Amazon sells more non-fiction than fiction, for instance.

Most people focus on their area of expertise and do not appreciate the value of using the 'soft' art of storytelling. Yet storytelling can lead to higher prices, increased margins, market dominance, more sales, better clients, and more people coming to you.

We can often design the best products globally and not sell them. The market is where people hear stories and connect. The trick is getting from nowhere to where you need to be.

You can always rely on a story to get to where you are going.

Disney, Marvel, Batman are examples of stories becoming industries. It can be done. Stories work miracles.

Chapter 23: Founder story conclusion

No doubt, things are different for you. Our stories will never be the same.

I lived south of London in the home counties, the middle of Surrey, when things kicked off for me. No doubt you live somewhere else. You may think living where I lived was privileged, maybe it was, maybe it was not. I had no choice in the matter, like millions of others, I had to make my own way. You do too.

I did not plan much of my journey; I had no rich uncles or worldly experience mentors to show me the way. I did, however, focus on my passions, and I wanted to do constructive, positive things. I was shocked when I realized I had got into missile guidance.

As a schoolboy and even at college, I had little appreciation of what happened in the big world.

About the military, I had only seen films about World War II, and we were always the winners. I was caught up in the winning story and thought working in defense was a good thing. It suited me at the time. I did my time. I'm happy to report I know nothing of that world now. Of course, saddened by what I see on TV. I am no conscientious objector. I simply do not work in defense electronics, that was decades ago.

Your story will be completely different. I hope you can see some of your own stories in mine, and you have felt inspired to write down a few bullet points to kick start your business storytelling. How would I be writing this if I was you may be a question that springs to mind. It depends on two things, the number of stories you have, which in turn probably relates to age.

The older you are, the more you will have witnessed, and the probability is you will have more stories to tell. I have known late starters do more in less time than me, and in one or two cases, die a lot younger than me as they took even less care of their health. I recall hearing from many people, possibly because I started so young 'well, you are young enough to recover' I heard it so often I thought at first it was a joke, then later it dawned on me what was being said. Few believed in me. I believed in myself. My self-belief is a bonus story!

However, I omitted many stories from this book. I have tried to edit these founder chapters so the stories I tell all relate to my experience of business development or growth. I could have included more stories from my earlier years, my time at school, at different places I lived, the different people, the different relationships, the different schools and later college, the people I met, what we did and then to win my apprenticeship (1 out of 500 applicants) and the subsequent studies and certifications achieved in later life undertaken on my own volition. I do use those stories and I am always finding new ways to relate them to business lessons. There are more.

I could have included all the stories and if you lack business experience, then you should and could tap into all of that has happened to you and more. I just happen to have more than enough actual business experience. Having the luxury to pick and choose means I have tried to pick those that are more meaningful for you.

Some people over the years have reacted poorly to some of my stories, expecting them to be bigger than they were. I certainly could have added creative license to boost them. They could have been juiced up, for sure. Believe me, living through them was enough. Many felt like they were out of the fire and then into frying pan situations. Many of them don't need to be big stories, as these are real everyday stories that really could happen, as they did to me.

I figured it is appropriate to make the points I wanted to make. As they appear as actual references in a book about business storytelling, they should, hopefully, resonate more. My plan is they should inspire you, too. Be afraid, but most importantly, be careful. While we should plan for the worst, reality is the worst rarely happens. Most things that look like they are going wrong, often get fixed, rarely do you have to wait until the last minute. But there will always be one time.

Chapter 24:
Last orders!

Much can be achieved in the pub! In the end, talking to people makes all the difference.

You can go to a pub without drinking it dry. Nowadays, you can order soft drinks in most places, including tea and coffee. I mention it because this may be where your customers are or where your fans congregate, you need to go there.

Who are your buyers?

The people most likely to buy are existing customers, secondly, there are past buyers, maybe equal to them are current and new fans. There may even be a group who are not fans at all but have a passing interest. They are all worth talking to. They may be in an ideal position to pass on information and refer others to you. They could well turn out to be a group of early adopters, or they may well hate you and everything you stand for. Either way, you need to know.

What are their stories?

You want to find out what their stories are, how did they get to be where they are? What do they like and don't they, beyond your product or service? If you had to amalgamate them into one homogeneous customer, what would he and she look like? What would their interests be? What would they wear? Do they have kids? Your objective must be to talk to them and bring them onside. For that, you need to get familiar with them and understand what drives them, so you can create stories to help them, so they recognize you are for them.

Your referral strategy?

Most enterprises have no referral strategy whatsoever.

However, most businesses get business by referral. They could get more. A simple solution is to create or commission an introduction pack. Your introduction pack would ideally be printed and very portable. You hand it over to those you meet and always carry a few copies on your person. Your introduction pack does not have to be large and outlandish; it just needs to be fit for purpose and handy.

I know this is a fact, as for many years I was the same. I would simply rely on about 20% of the business coming in by referral. I would refer to it as the Bluebird business. The idea was that Bluebirds would fly through our windows. It was magic. 20% of our business came that way that we knew of.

It took me years to realize my colleagues were expert networkers and they were very well known in the industry. It was their connections that brought many clients. There were also many client staff moving from one place to another and the services my business offered were their secret weapons. We did well with it. Did we only do 20% or was it really 80%? We could have done a whole lot better if we had reviewed this earlier and worked on a plan of action. What story should we tell and how should we tell them?

Innovation and referral strategies are both processes. In another one of my books, 'How To Start A Business Without Any Money', I refer to the need to create automatic assets. These are, in effect, assets you can spin off and create, usually for free, using the resources you already have. Both the processes of Innovation and Referral can be spun into no-cost assets and easily added to a business.

As processes are assets, you can value them on a balance sheet and show them as intellectual property and provide them as part of the reason why a business will succeed. They form the basis of how the business can grow and spin off subsidiaries. They will help you sell your business. Assets of this type are especially valuable.

The great news is that you can either develop these kinds of assets yourself or work with your team and have your team work on them out for you. Often, I hear of senior managers and directors instructing or trying to induce the staff to be more innovative, to add innovation to the enterprise, which is a really good idea, although useless if no one, including the manager, knows how to innovate.

You do not necessarily have to improve or add any new products. You can simply describe them in different ways, you can change the pricing, you can update and improve the packages, and the descriptions or application areas for your service or products. Most of what you need to do is to find new ways to look at what you offer and specially to see them through the eyes of your clientele.

One of my favorites, most revealing, and fastest ways to grow a business is simply to talk about the improvements or additions to what you provide to clients and to listen to their ideas. Most will say they want it faster, cheaper, of course, and you can ask in what way, what should be faster, where can they see opportunities for reducing cost? Some will be able to tell you, others will not, but most will be glad you are paying attention.

Chances are your best clients will tell you what they want in more detail, what they use you for, what they achieve with you and how you might deliver more value for them. They may even talk themselves into buying more or paying more as you realize you can customize your delivery to suit them better and, in the process, tie them ever closer to you and further away from your competitors.

Finally, if you have been writing every day

You should have seen your writing evolve, the quality of writing, the speed of writing and the ideas themselves change and mature since you have been writing. If you write every day and publish on Twitter, you can also see the stats every day. Most bloggers blog once a month, so in a month, if you have published every day, you will have more stats than most bloggers have collected in a year – and you will not have bothered to build up a blog, as publishing on Twitter means you are publishing to a massive audience immediately. After a month, you should have started to notice at least some feedback and picked up some followers along the way too.

Comments will be shared, questions asked and answered, likes, views and shares. It will not be earth shattering, but if one post has one like and another two, that is a large, 100% difference. Although the numbers may be insignificant, the indications may well be positive and, if you are lucky, one post may have even gone viral.

So, a month later, your writing will have improved, your approach has matured, you are probably down to 15 minutes or more to produce a quick article and you probably have more content ideas than ever before. Keep going write for fifteen minutes every day. Your ability to produce stories and run them across different media will keep improving and, all in all, you will find you are the subject authority figure.

This is an outstanding achievement and represents the next area of your growth. I am planning for the topic of authority figure to be the focus of my next book. If this topic interests you, make sure to sign up for my free newsletter https://theauthorityfigure.substack.com/ and I will point you in the right direction ahead of time.

I hope you have enjoyed reading this book. Would you please leave a review on Amazon at https://www.amazon.com/dp/B09XVLSZ6C/ and tell us your story (see chapter 5 for a straightforward framework). Reviews help other readers find the book. You would provide a great service to this author and future readers. Thank you.